A New Horse For Marny

◆

Libby Anderson
Illustrated by Heather St. Clair Davis

Half Halt Press, Inc.
Boonsboro, Maryland

Editor's Note

In bringing this delightful book to a new audience outside Australia where it was originally published, we had a major decision to make. Since our English and Australian English are sometimes quite different, should we change all the spellings, like "colour" to "color", explain things like how Christmas in Australia falls in the summer rather than winter, and define terms, like a "float" is a horse trailer?

We decided no, figuring that all the meanings are clear from the context anyway and, besides, all the differences are part of the flavor of Marny's world.

Yes, there are differences in how we might say something, or how we'd spell it, but we all share Marny's emotions and feelings, her desire to learn more about the art of horsemanship, and her love for her horse – wherever we live on the planet.

This story is dedicated to Franz Mairinger,
in appreciation of his efforts to
stimulate the classical art of riding
throughout Australia.

Chapter 1

Marny swung open the stable door and carefully latched it back before leading Sure Smile into the yard. The pony stepped lightly across the gutter, pricking her ears forward—perhaps the scent of other horses was coming to her across the breeze. Her small dark hooves clattered on the paving stones as she pranced, whinnying with pleasure to be outside.

When Marny's father, Sigismund Mann, had bought the house eighteen years before, the stable yard and its adjoining paddock were all that remained of the original farm. Her parents preferred the old house with all its inconveniences to a modern building, and Marny loved it too—at least there was sufficient grazing for her pony and enough space to put up her home-made jumps.

"I must be the luckiest girl in Australia to have *you,*" Marny told the mare, twining the long silvery forelock through her fingers. Sure Smile ignored her owner's caresses and nudged her hand.

"I can take a hint," said Marny, producing an apple from the pocket of her jeans. The mare took the titbit delicately, then lowered her head to have her ears scratched. Cradling her mare's head in her arms, the girl stayed daydreaming for several minutes. Then she said decisively, "If I don't start work soon, we'll never be through." Sure Smile's head was already hanging in a resigned fashion. She knew it was time for her Saturday-morning shampoo. It was humiliating for a horse whose ancestors had raced across the desert in war bands, thundered down the turf at Newmarket, and carried Irish chieftains safely through bogs and across mountains, to be covered completely in soapy bubbles from her poll to her fetlocks.

Marny did not use soap on Sure Smile, but "borrowed" her mother's best shampoo. Poor Trudy Mann could never understand why each bottle was finished so quickly. As Marny slowly hosed off the bubbles, she was suddenly drenched in soapy water by a flick of Sure Smile's wet tail. But she worked on, rubbing, rinsing, drying, and finally brushing until the pony looked as if she had just stepped out of a cellophane box instead of a stable, with a coat of real silk instead of horsehair. Her long tail was silvery grey with some white hairs and some black. Marny had combed it until it flowed thick and straight down to her fetlocks. She kept the pony tied up for an hour until she was completely dry and then released her into the small paddock behind the stable yard. Sure Smile trotted out, her silvery mane and tail streaming like banners in the wind. Then, to pay Marny back for the humiliation of the shampoo, she deliberately lay down and rolled and rolled until she had covered the result of hours of patient work in a patina of fine dust. Marny closed her eyes in pretended horror.

"At least you're clean underneath, and it'll all brush off tomorrow."

The pony got up and began to frisk round the paddock, cantering and bucking in circles, like a filly instead of a sensible six-year-old in training for her second show season. Tomorrow was the annual district show, but Marny had forced herself not to think about it. Sure Smile came readily to her whistle. Marny stabled her and gave her the evening feed, after which she tied up the hay-net and put the stable in order.

"Have you finished, darling?" asked her mother. Trudy Mann knew nothing about horses, but she loved to see her daughter happy. Marny sat on the kitchen table swinging her legs nonchalantly, pretending a calm she did not feel.

"Sure Smile will look terrific, Mum." She gave her plump mother a quick peck on the cheek. "Everything will be O.K." But inside her stomach she felt the first flutterings of nervous

2

butterflies. That wasn't unusual on a preshow day, but this time there was also a strange premonition that something would go wrong.

The telephone rang and her mother called out, "For you, Marianne." Marny ran and picked up the receiver. The friendly, familiar voice of her best friend, Candida Thomas, came through as clearly as if she were in the room.

"How do you feel about tomorrow, Marny? I've just put Moonlight in. He's rolled all over his shampoo."

"Sure Smile did too."

"Aren't you excited? I am."

"No, I'm not. I feel awful. I don't want to go."

"Oh, Marny! You're always the same before a big show. Then you go in and win. You did last year. You beat Alice in the Novice Jumping and got three firsts."

"I know I did. I *do* want to win—for Sure Smile more than for me. I'm so lucky to have her. I want to show everyone how much she can do. I feel so responsible for her. There's Mr.. Oliver and Mark, the Shooter's...."

"I'm glad I don't have to show Moonlight off to anyone," laughed Candida. "Now stop worrying—and get a good night's sleep."

"You sound just like Mum. I will. But....there's something else. I don't know....it seems silly even to tell you."

"What is it?"

"I've got this funny feeling about the show. Something terrible will happen."

"Funny ha-ha, you mean! Don't be silly. What *can* happen?"

Marny put the receiver down gently and went slowly into her bedroom. She remembered Sure Smile cantering gaily round the paddock. As Candy had said, what could possibly go wrong? She decided not to worry any longer.

4

Chapter 2

Marny was up at five o'clock to feed the mare. They had an eight-kilometre trek to the showground, and she wanted to be there early. She was too nervous and excited to want any breakfast herself, but Sure Smile, who was a greedy animal, chomped her oats with gusto. After every few mouthfuls she would stop chewing and turn her beautiful eyes on Marny as if to say, "What, aren't you hungry?" Marny wasn't. The few butterflies in her stomach yesterday had grown into a whole host of fluttering insects, but she knew that if she didn't go up to the house and pretend to eat something, her father would say, "There you are, Trudy, I keep telling you the child's overwrought. She won't eat. This horse business is *bad* for her." To avoid that familiar scene, Marny sat down with her parents and forced herself to eat cereal and toast. Whisky, her Corgi, sat tactfully under her feet to be fed most of the toast when her father wasn't looking. Whisky had been given to her on her tenth birthday, and they were devoted to each other.

"What are your plans for today, Sigi?" Trudy asked.

"*Ach.* I have to go to see those children with measles. There are so many spotted children in this town I begin to think I have optical delusions. But I know what you are driving to....I will come this afternoon and see *Liebchen* jump."

"Oh, Dad, I'm glad." Marny hugged him, knowing her father disliked her riding. He'd been a brilliant surgeon in Vienna before the second World War, then imprisonment and torture in a Nazi concentration camp had ruined his hands. And now he wanted his only daughter to follow the career barred to him. But Marny didn't want to be a surgeon—or even a doctor. If she couldn't work professionally with horses, she wanted to be a vet.

Marny was early at the showground, and as she walked her pony carefully to the competitors' stalls, she saw that only a few horses had arrived. The first person she recognised was Alice Shooter. Alice's father ran the local riding school, and Alice competed at all the local shows with Mirabelle, her chestnut Thoroughbred. Alice usually won all her classes and was becoming conceited.

Marny smiled at her rival. "Hello," she called. "I'll put Sure Smile next to Mirabelle." Alice looked scornfully at Sure Smile and jerked Mirabelle's bridle roughly. Mirabelle threw up her head and started backing out of the stall.

"Stop that, you brute." Alice jerked the bridle again. "Can't you settle your pony, Marny? She's upsetting mine. It's all very well for you with a part-bred. But Thoroughbreds are highly strung and nervous. Do hurry up." Alice was so unpleasant that Marny began to feel nervous herself. Then she saw that Candida had arrived, and waved vigorously in order to attract her attention.

Candida rode up on Moonlight, a thickset black cob. Girl and pony were both seventeen years old, and although Moonlight was reaching the end of his working life and Candida's was just beginning, they made a well-matched pair. Both were plump, both were cheerful, and both had an over-developed sense of mischief.

"Hello Marny. Hello Alice. Doesn't Sure Smile look beautiful? Don't you wish *you* were as beautiful, Alice?"

Alice glared at the innocently smiling, dark-eyed Candida and stalked off to find her father. Moonlight attempted to say "Hello" to Mirabelle and nearly got kicked.

"Can't you kids keep your ponies in order?" Alice called back over her shoulder.

Marny's face flushed.

"Take no notice of her," said Candida quickly. "She's eaten up with jealousy—that's why she's being so nasty."

The first event in which the two friends were to take part was "Girl Rider (14 to 18 years)." They prepared together, putting the final touches to the ponies' grooming. Candida produced an old silk scarf from her pocket and proceeded to polish both animals.

"Dad said the grooms used to do this in England in the old days. Silk brings up the shine."

Marny felt sick as they walked towards the arena, but at the actual moment of entering the ring she forgot about herself and concentrated on showing off her pony to her best advantage. The Girl Rider was a quiet, ladylike affair, and Marny found it calmed her down. Besides Sure Smile, Moonlight, and Mirabelle, there were four ponies from Alex Shooter's riding school, and various mounts ridden by a handful of local girls. The best-looking was a bright bay horse ridden by a girl from the neighbouring town, but she was eliminated quite early when one of the spectators opened a beer can right under the horse's nose. The poor animal got such a fright that he reared up and tore off across the ring, and by the time he was under control and back in the arena, the judges had waved the girl out.

"Bad luck," Marny whispered, as the handsome bay trotted past, tossing his head and looking unashamed. Alice looked relieved to see his departure, which left Mirabelle and Sure Smile as the only quality horses.

The judges now called the competitors in and asked them to canter a circle on the right rein. Marny gave the aids a little clumsily and Sure Smile cantered a few strides on the wrong lead. Alice smiled superciliously before she executed the movement, sitting beautifully erect on her show saddle, all her tack in perfect order. She took the first prize, Marny came second, and one of the Shooter ponies was third. The three girls looked immaculate as they cantered round the ring with their rosettes on the ponies' bridles. Nobody noticed that Alice's winning smile was a little too triumphant. Marny still had the funny feeling that something awful was going to happen. "I must stop worrying," she thought. "It's so silly."

As the girls rode back towards the stables they were stopped by a loud "Hi, Marny. You looked fabulous." Blair Morse was

7

beaming with pleasure. He was the local high school football star, worshipped by far too many girls: perhaps that was the reason he wanted only Marny, who was cool and shy and seemed to prefer horses. Occasionally, Blair was able to persuade her to go out with him to the pictures or to a school dance. He had even taken up riding at Shooter's establishment to try to please her.

"Thanks, Blair," said Marny. "We must go now, Candy's folks have arrived."

"Why don't you boys join us for lunch?" Candida asked. Blair was with a university friend of his, Barry Dalson, whom Candy had been keen on for ages.

"Great," said Blair, still looking admiringly at Marny. "We'd love to."

"What's next for you?" asked Barry, as the four of them started untacking the ponies.

Marny consulted her show programme. "Nothing until after lunch. Candy and I are riding in the Pairs together."

"O. K.," said Blair. "Let's go and join your folks. Think they'll have enough to go round?"

"Wait and see," laughed Candida.

No one could miss the arrival of the Thomas brothers and their families. They settled down in ringside seats, talking and laughing. Although Mark Thomas, the local vet, was childless, his brother Andrew was the opposite: his wife, Janey, was only happy when she had a baby to hold. There were already five children, of whom Candida was the oldest. The last baby, Micky, was almost out of nappies, and Janey was looking broody again. Andrew, secretly proud of his large family, threatened to divorce her if she had any more. Marny picked up the baby by the seat of his pants and gave him a quick hug. Sometimes she envied the bustle and confusion of Candida's home, so different from the calm orderliness of her own.

"And Candy never has any trouble over her riding," she thought. Indeed, Andrew never minded what the children did as long as they left him in peace.

"Moonlight looks fit, Mr. Thomas," Barry said.

"Doesn't he? Funny to think we've had him since Marny and Candida were kids. How time flies."

8

"Do you remember, Dad," said young Paul Thomas, "when Moonie threw Mrs. Rowbotham into the brambles 'cos she was yanking his head and saying, "Boy, oh boy, ain't this great," and bouncing on his kidneys?"

"Yes, and I remember apologising to her because you lot were laughing too much to pull her out."

Janey tactfully changed the subject by opening the picnic hamper. Mark Thomas and his Greek wife Melissa joined them, and they were followed by Marny's parents. The three Manns were quieter than the Thomas clan, but they made a gay party all the same. Marny stopped worrying and began to look forward to the afternoon's jumping.

Lunch was soon over for the two girls. "Come on Marny. They're calling the Pairs."

Chapter 3

There were only five pairs competing, and Marny was almost sure of a place if Moonlight could take the larger hurdles in his stride. Around the long sides of the arena eight batten fences were placed, four to a side. The pairs had to steeplechase the fences together. Teamwork was the most important factor. Checking Sure Smile's faster pace, Marny kept her jumping in perfect unison with the black gelding. Candida's face grew pink with excitement as they cleared the course. Only at the second-to-last jump, Moonlight faltered and knocked the fence–but it was too heavy to fall. The judge tied the yellow ribbon around the cob's thick neck.

Now came the great test for Marny and Sure Smile. Last season, the grey pony had jumped her way out of the novice classes, so today they were to face the Open Olympic, where the competition was beyond the ability of Candida's aged cob.

"Good luck," said Candida. "I'm glad it's not me out there. The course looks tough."

"It is."

As Marny walked the course, she felt her confidence returning. Sure Smile could do it. She had been sailing over the fences in the Pairs and was still fresh and eager. Marny was a late draw and would be jumping almost last, before Alice Shooter, so now she and Candida sat on the white boundary rails to watch the other competitors. Nine horses had completed their rounds before Marny legged-up on Sure Smile. The difficult layout of the fences had taken its toll, and there had been only one clear round so far—the girl who had been eliminated from the Girl Rider in the morning. The steward called Marny over. She saluted the judge, heard the bell, and set off for her round. Now she was oblivious of the crowd, of her fears, of her appearance. She was aware only of the controlled power beneath her and the jumps laid out before her.

Sure Smile pricked up her ears as her eyes focused on each jump. "Don't worry," she might have been telling her rider. "We've been training for this for a year. It's my work and I love it." Her timing and rhythm were near-perfect today, and Marny felt that she and the animal were one being. The water jump was long and effortless. Marny sent the mare at the combination jump at threequarter pace, and Sure Smile took it easily—one long stride and out again over the spread. The last jump, a "road closed," was safely cleared and then they cantered through the finishing flags. Marny heard the cheers from the crowd as she drew Sure Smile back to a trot and patted her damp neck.

As she heard the bell, Alice turned Mirabelle with a sharp jag in the mouth which must have hurt the little Thoroughbred. But she was a game mare and put up with the punishment Alice gave her. She plunged forward, upset and excited. Marny felt sorry for her, but the crowd cheered Alice's showy performance. Mirabelle steadied at the approach to the first jump and was safely over. Now came the tricky water jump. "Too fast, too fast," thought Marny. But the mare cleared it, tucking up her heels and landing neatly. Over the hogsback, and now the combination. Alice checked Mirabelle too much: she took off early for the first element and then, when it seemed impossible, took an immense leap forward over the second—a spread—and cleared it by a hairsbreadth. Marny breathed again. "What a jump!" The crowd gave Alice a loud cheer.

There were now three horses left in for the jump-off. The course was shortened by three obstacles, and the remaining jumps were raised. The round was to be run on time against the clock. The crowd was large for a local show, for this was the most exciting event of the day. The first horse, the pretty bay, was unlucky and knocked the top rail off the hogsback. As he landed, he pecked and slid to his knees. The crowd oohed and aahed. With an immense effort he stood up and continued his round to loud cheers. But the fall had knocked many seconds off his time.

The bell sounded for Marny's round. She took a quick decision. She would try for a clear round but not take the course very fast. She and Sure Smile weren't experienced enough yet. If Mirabelle followed at a faster pace, that couldn't be helped. The first part of the combination was up to 140 centimetres, and Sure Smile cleared it, agile as a cat. She had powerful jumping quarters and a cool head. Now Marny's hours of patient schooling were showing results. The mare jumped everything in sight as calmly as though she were in her home paddock. Over the last jump—the "road closed"—and then Marny let her out in a fast sprint between the flags. The crowd was delighted. The announcer commented on "this promising pair" and forecast "a great future" for them both. Candida ran up to help Marny dismount.

"There goes the bell for Alice's round. This is it," she said.

Marny could not take her eyes off Mirabelle. The little mare flew along, cutting corners.

"She's certainly out to beat your time," said Candida.

The mare was jumping boldly but becoming increasingly flustered as Alice used her whip continually. Up to the last fence the mare was flying, but in the end the tension became too great for her. Instead of clearing the final jump, she appeared not to see it and blundered straight through. It rocked and fell. Alice slashed Mirabelle across the ears. The cheering crowd began to boo. Alice, furious, did not even notice. The judge cautioned her for cruelty and waved her out. She obeyed sulkily.

"Look after that mare of yours," the judge told Marny as he tied the winning ribbon round Sure Smile's neck. "I'm expecting to see a great deal more of you both."

Marny nodded, too proud and happy to speak.

Back at the stables, two pairs of hands enthusiastically rubbed down Sure Smile and she was left nibbling at her hay-net as calmly as though she won three ribbons every day. All the Thomas family congratulated Marny. Mark Thomas could not resist saying to Sigi, "Didn't I tell you that filly would be a winner?"

13

"What if you did?" replied Sigi. But he, too, was delighted.

Marny didn't enjoy all the fuss. "Let's go home now, Candy. Or we won't get there before dark."

"O.K., Winner," laughed Candida, knowing why her friend was anxious to leave. "I'll ride with you as far as the turn-off."

The girls packed up quickly. As they brought out the ponies, ready to mount, they saw the Shooter float with its ramp down, surrounded by horses and ponies. Each animal wore a smart monogrammed rug.

"Congratulations, my dear," Alex Shooter called out. He had allowed Marny to use his jumps for training and had occasionally instructed her, and so he felt that her success was partly due to him, even though she had not been one of his paying pupils. "Well ridden! I might let you jump for me next season."

"Thanks, Mr. Shooter, but I'll be busy with Sure Smile."

"Well, you never know, do you? If you change your mind...."

"I won as many ribbons as she did," Alice mumbled sulkily.

"*What* did you say?" Hard-headed as he was, Alex disliked his daughter's poor sportsmanship. "Haven't you congratulated Marny yet?"

"Why should I?"

"Go and do it *now*." Alex hissed the words at her between his teeth, and Alice knew better than to disobey. Pulling poor Mirabelle roughly behind her, she walked over to Marny, whose foot was already in the stirrup as she prepared to mount. Mirabelle was still sweating from nervous fatigue. As Alice opened her mouth to speak there was a loud report from the exhaust of a passing car. The over-excited chestnut reared, jerking the reins from Alice's hand; then, turning to gallop off, she put her head down and gave an almighty buck. Her left hind shoe caught Sure Smile hard behind the ear. The blow pushed the grey sideways and Marny was flung to the ground. Half-stunned, Sure Smile staggered out into the road. A four-tonne float was coming out fast round the stables, and the dazed mare crashed headlong into its side.

Marny screamed. And then she saw everything happen slowly, as if in a nightmare. Her premonitions had come true. Scrambling to her feet, she saw Sure Smile's leg lying at an

14

impossible angle and blood staining the ground as it spurted out from a wound in her chest. The driver of the float backed it off, then leapt out and came running over, white faced and shaking. "I couldn't help it," he muttered. "I couldn't help it. She walked straight into me."

Marny knelt and cradled the mare's head in her arms — all that bright beauty an insignificant bundle lying in the dirt.

"I am sorry. I *really* am," said Alice. Perhaps she was; but Marny never heard.

Within minutes, Mark Thomas was beside them, staunching the blood from the chest wound.

"It looks bad, Marny," he said gently. The perfect professional in a crisis, his face showed no sign of emotion. "I'm going to give her a pain-killing injection."

Marny nodded. Carefully Mark filled the syringe and guided the needle into the jugular vein. As the anaesthetic began to circulate in her bloodstream, the mare's taut muscles relaxed, and in a few seconds she was unconscious.

"You know we have to take her away, don't you?"

Marny nodded again. Tears ran unchecked down her cheeks. Gently she laid the mare's head on the ground, stroked the shut eyes, and kissed the soft muzzle. The winning ribbons were still in her hand. She put them down too.

"They weren't worth it," she said. The bystanders watched as she walked slowly away into the bush. Candida started to follow her.

"Let her go alone," said Sigi. He had arrived in time to see the body being lifted by a crane on to a float and now he and Mark stood in silence, watching it trundle out of sight with the unconscious mare aboard. Everyone went home. Sure Smile's ribbons were left on the ground, a brightly coloured heap, in the fast-falling dusk.

15

Chapter 4

The weeks following the accident seemed endless. Marny became scared of people, of sympathy, or any friendly gesture. She did not want anyone to mention Sure Smile or to ask what had happened at the show. Since that evening, she had not seen Mark or even telephoned to ask the vet where the float had been taken. At times she forgot the accident and found herself walking down to the pony's stable as though nothing had happened. Her parents watched her misery helplessly. Sigismund considered buying another horse, but knew that he could not afford a replacement for Sure Smile, so, watching his daughter pick listlessly at her food or sit staring silently at the empty paddock, he never even suggested it. Straight after tea each evening Marny disappeared with Whisky, not saying where she was going. Her parents guessed that she must have spent the time wandering along the bush paths she knew so well, grieving for her dead pony.

"We can do nothing but wait until she needs us," Sigi told his wife. "Time heals everything."

Marny found school unbearable at first, full of friendly, anxious faces that she could not avoid. But as the days passed, school became her greatest comfort. She started to study hard, concentrating on mathematical problems and filling her mind with facts. Her school marks became what Sigismund had hoped for, but the look in his daughter's eyes was too high a price to pay for them.

Marny couldn't stop herself remembering. She had always said that she didn't believe in fate, and she never read her horoscope in magazines. Yet if it wasn't fate, destiny, or *something*, then how could an ordinary girl like her ever have come to own Sure Smile? "Maybe," she thought, "I wasn't good enough for her."

For Marny, shy, clumsy, and too tall, thought very little of herself. But she wasn't ordinary. Mark Thomas had discovered this very early, when Marny had been a little girl in pigtails, and she and Candida used to haunt his surgery. For Marny had a natural gift: she could calm frightened animals. She was unafraid of them. Once, as an eleven-year-old, she had led an escaped bull back into his pen when none of the men dared approach him. Marny helped Mark in his work with dogs and cats, and whenever she was allowed she climbed into his station wagon and went out with him to properties where he treated horses, sheep, and cattle. Candida always refused to come too. "No thanks," she used to say. "Too much blood for me."

Through Mark Thomas, Candida and Marny got their first pony.

A farmer had given it, worn-out and unwanted, to Mark. "Sell him or shoot him," he was told. But Mark soon found that neglect, not old age, had caused the trouble. The pony's teeth were so overgrown that he could not graze properly. One back molar had pierced the gum and made an abscess which caused acute pain each time he tried to chew. After his teeth had been filed and his worms cured, he quickly regained condition. The dull yellow coat fell out in handfuls, and the pony finally emerged as a bright bay with a yellow mane and tail. He was called Sunshine, or Small Miracle, because every time Melissa, Mark's wife, saw him she used to say, "Praise the Lord. He has performed a small miracle."

Mark gave Sunshine to the two girls, and the mischievous pony taught them all the tricks of the trade. It made Marny giggle to remember his bad habits. He had taught the girls better than any expensive riding school would have done. They had to sit firmly in the saddle or Sunny would buck them off and trot away, leaving the bruised rider to walk home. They had to use their legs to *push* the pony on, or else he would never emerge from an ambling trot. For he was born idle and considered his time best spent dozing in the paddock.

Marny grew too tall for Sunshine, but her father refused to buy a bigger pony. Sigi Mann didn't approve of all this messing around with animals. He had other, grander ambitions for his only child. But short of tying her up in her bedroom, nothing could keep her away from animals—any animals, but especially horses.

"I expect she'll grow out of it," Marny's mother told her husband. "I'm sure girls lose interest in such things when they grow up a bit and want to be young ladies." But Marny grew even taller, until she looked like an awkward filly herself, and still spent all her free time at the vet's or the riding stables, or jumping the too-small Sunny. But the time came when, sitting astride her pony, her feet almost touched the ground; and she knew then that Sunshine had earned his reward — a comfortable retirement in a sheltered paddock.

Soon after this, Andrew Thomas, much less fussy about horses than Marny's father, had bought Candida a black cob. They called him Moonlight. He was a jolly animal and he suited his new owner, who was not horsemad like Marny. It seemed to Marny that she would never have another pony. But one winter's night, the second miracle happened.

Naturally Marny had heard of Peter Oliver, for he bred the finest ponies and light horses in the district. Mr. Oliver had spent many years trying to breed the perfect pony. There are 35000 active pony-club members in Australia, and he wanted a good share of that profitable market. He experimented by crossing Anglo-Arabs with Connemaras, to produce a pony combining the gaiety and endurance of the Arab, the temperament and jumping ability of the Connemara, and the quality of the Thoroughbred. His ambitious venture was gradually succeeding. Marny had often seen his brood mares and their foals in the paddocks and admired them from a distance. She could never have dreamed of owning one. Then, a few months later, her luck changed.

It was a terrible winter's night. Gale-force winds whipped branches from elms and gum trees so that they crashed to the

19

ground with boughs splintering, blocking roads and making dams in the creeks. Rain mixed with hail bruised the face of anyone mad enough or unlucky enough to be outside. Flashes of lightning showed up flocks of sodden sheep patiently waiting out the storm.

On this wild night a mare was foaling down, not in the open paddock, but in a clean, comfortable foaling-box filled with fresh straw. Rain and hail tattooed on the galvanised-iron roof of her stable as she strained and panted. She was in great trouble. The foetus was turned the wrong way round and the mare, already exhausted, could not push the tiny foal from her womb. Sweat was running off her flanks and her eyes were filmy. Clearly, unless help came soon, she would be finished.

Peter Oliver was on the telephone to Mark Thomas, his voice trembling over the crackling wires.

"Mark, you must do something or I shall lose them both."

"Steady down," came the calm reply. "Tell me how she is."

As he listened to the anxious voice, Mark realised how grave the situation was.

"She needs an immediate Caesarean operation if we are to save them."

"You can't make it! The roads are blocked."

"Don't worry. Keep the mare as calm as you can. I'll be there within the hour." The line went dead, and Peter Oliver was left to wait and hope.

"Melissa," Mark called out to his wife as he picked up his bag. "Trouble at the Oliver place. I'll have to ride Pye over."

Melissa knew that it was useless to try to dissuade him, so with a quiet "Take care of yourself," she helped him to prepare. As she did so, she silently repeated to herself a prayer in her native Greek, for Mark was no expert horseman. His steady piebald gelding was kept only for Sunday hacks and occasional driving. However, as Mark led the animal into the blinding gale, Pye stepped out unhesitatingly. He struggled on the iced-up roads, but he never fell, even when he had to ford the fast-flowing creeks full of fallen timber.

"Not long now," Mark whispered, urging Pye into a faster trot along the final stretch—a short dirt track which led to the

Oliver property. He had avoided as many roads as possible and cut across country, saving eight kilometres. True to his word, he was in the yard within the hour. His task completed, Pye stood trembling, steam rising from his soaking coat, but soon he was inside a warm box and a strapper belonging to the stud was rubbing him down and giving him a warm bran mash.

Meanwhile Mark prepared to operate, with Peter Oliver as his assistant. The mare was strong and young: this was her third foal. The operation was going well, when there was a sudden crash of falling timbers. The wind had blown down the power lines, plunging the stable in total darkness.

"Hold still," Oliver cried out. "Tom! Tom!" The strapper knew immediately what to do. Groping his way to the tack room, he lit two hurricane lamps, and the operation continued under their flickering beams.

Finally Mark lifted the still, wet body from the opening he had made in the mare's side and handed the foal to Peter Oliver. Oliver held it carefully, his eyes tired from straining in the dim light. They brightened as the foal stirred. It was a chestnut filly.

"Mark, I think I've done it. She's perfect!"

"Of course," came the curt reply. "But let's see to the mare."

Oliver sensed the rebuke. He placed the foal on a thick mat, covered her with a hessian bag, and turned to the mother. Heavily anaesthetised, the mare was breathing regularly, unaware of her baby beside her.

"Pass the blunt-nosed forceps," Mark ordered. He sutured the incision through which he had withdrawn the foal, and closed the wound. Now it was his turn to relax.

Up at the house, over mugs of brandy-laced tea, the breeder could hardly stop thanking the vet. He was light-headed with relief. "It isn't just for *my* stud, you see. That mare is one of the best Connemaras in the country. I imported her three years ago. It's with mares like that that we're going to put Australian ponies on the map."

Peter Oliver knew that Mark would never accept any extra fee for what he had done, so he thought of a plan to reward him. A few days later, he persuaded the vet to accept one of his young stock as a gift. Mark chose a dapple-grey filly and called her Sure Smile.

Sure Smile had been a late foal and, being less well developed than her brothers and sisters, had not been sold as a two-year-old. At three years she was showing the quality of her breeding. Her dam was the grey Connemara whose life Mark had saved, and her sire an Anglo-Arab who counted the royal blood of desert Arabians in his bloodlines. Mark, childless himself, immediately gave her to Marny; and that was how the thirteen-year-old girl came to own one of the best ponies in the country.

March drew into April and with it came cooler winds whipped up from the south-east. One Friday afternoon Marny came home from school and found Trudy peeling potatoes in the kitchen. Pulling out the three-legged milking stool from under the table, she sat astride it and began to talk about Sure Smile. As she talked, she began to cry and finally to babble incoherently as she let out all the pent-up emotions of the last weeks. When she had stopped crying Trudy led her to her bedroom and put her to bed as if she was still a small child. For the first night since the show, Marny's dreams were free of the sound of galloping hooves and the vision of a dying mare. She woke up late on Saturday morning feeling hungry. Sigismund was at home, for he had stayed in on purpose after Trudy had told him the good news. He brought in a tray of coffee and her favourite cake and found Marny lying in bed with Whisky curled up in the crook of her arm.

"What's all this, Dad? It's not my birthday." Her father smiled and patted her hand. At last she was able to talk to him, and they felt closer to one another than they had been since Marny was a baby.

"I'm very proud of you, Marny. You've accepted the facts at last."

"I know there can never be another Sure Smile," Marny replied simply. "I was just so lucky to have had her at all."

"That's the right spirit, *Liebchen*. I wish I could afford another horse of that class. But I can't."

Marny nodded and looked out through her bedroom window over the empty paddock.

"What do you want to do now?" asked her father.

"For a start, I'd like to go with Mark on his rounds again. And Dad....I'll go on working hard at school, like you've always wanted me to."

"Marny, do you want to resume riding at Alex Shooter's? I can afford that, at least."

"I don't know, Dad. Can I think about it?"

"Of course. You know, love, if you really want to be a vet instead of a doctor, I won't oppose you."

"I know you won't. I wish I did want to be a doctor. But I just don't."

"Let's keep things as they are, Marny," Sigi said. "You've had a terrible shock and you've come through. Now you must pick up again." With that he kissed her and left.

Lunch that day was a family celebration, interrupted in the middle by a telephone call which Sigi answered, thinking that it might have been one of his patients. But it wasn't.

"Marny, that was Mark. There's an emergency call over at the Roberts place—a sick cow. I told him you'd go along to help. He'll be here straightaway."

Marny got up immediately. "Of course I'll go, Dad. I'm better now."

Her parents smiled happily at her impetuous departure.

Chapter 5

The station wagon bounced over the rutted dirt road as Mark tried to avoid potholes. Its best days were long past. When she had been a little girl and the wagon was new, Marny had painted "Waltzing Matilda" on the tailboard. Recently, someone had drawn a red line through "Waltzing" and scrawled "Limping" instead. "Limping Matilda" lurched onwards, broad paddocks stretching away on either side of her. This was cattle country: sleek-rumped Herefords sheltered under the gum trees, unconcerned as their fat calves drank from their mothers' ample teats or fought mock battles with each other. On the other side of the road, the rye and clover pasture was cropped shorter by a flock of sheep.

"Look at those superb fleeces, Marny," said Mark, pointing them out to her. "That's what people mean when they say Australia lives on the sheep's back."

Marny drew a deep breath of cool air through the open car window. "This is better than city life, isn't it, Mark? You have no time to think there, and everyone's in a rush."

"You know my view. If I didn't love the country I wouldn't be here. I'd have a fashionable Sydney practice dealing with fat rich ladies and their fat rich lapdogs." They laughed at the idea. Mark was far too plain-speaking to succeed at that.

"But Mark, Mum and Dad don't think the way we do. They often tell stories of their life in Vienna before the war, and I know they believe that things were better for them then. But

I'm just not very interested. I feel mean about it sometimes. I hate hurting their feelings, because they're so kind. They think I'm provincial. Maybe so. Maybe things *are* different in other places. But they couldn't be better. At least, not for me."

"If that's how you feel, you stick to it. Your parents will understand eventually."

The Roberts property was a wooden homestead, one of the earliest in the district. The original house had been rebuilt, but the old dairy still stood, leaning at a crazy angle against the hillside. The cows had been milked and put out to pasture, all except for some of the calves and the sick cow which Mark had come to tend.

"What happened?" Mark was already examining her.

"Dunno," replied Mr. Roberts. "We found her two days back. She's been bitten badly—wild dogs, I 'spect—and cut, on barbed wire."

"Why the hell wasn't I called earlier?" Mark asked angrily. The cow's wounds had turned septic and he feared blood-poisoning.

"It's hard to do the right thing at times," sighed old Roberts despondently. Mark nodded, wishing that he hadn't criticised. Roberts was not a wealthy farmer, and he had an extravagant wife and son. He couldn't afford too many veterinary bills.

Marny helped Mark lay out his instruments. He would have to suture the worst of the cuts. As she did so, she imagined how the accident must have happened. One of the several packs of ownerless, half-wild "town" dogs which roamed the countryside had probably chased the cow's calf through the rusty perimeter fence. The mother, fierce in her desire to protect her offspring, would have followed them, ripping open her dew-lap and tearing her belly on the jagged wire. She must have chased the snarling pack, repeatedly charging at them until they melted away into the hills, leaving only a badly wounded animal lowing softly for her tired and frightened calf.

"How I hate barbed wire," thought Marny, remembering many similar injuries she had seen. When Mark had finished suturing he gave the cow an antibiotic injection. "I'll telephone tomorrow and see how she is," he told Roberts.

Marny waited for Mark to finish, sitting astride an old wattle tree that must have been blown down years ago. The bark felt solid and almost alive beneath her thighs, and her hands absently caressed the rough bark. The breeze lightly lifted her hair and blew it across her face.

"Come on, old girl, we're off." Mark's hand rested on her shoulder.

"Sorry." She jumped up, startled. "I was miles away." As they clambered into the car, the farmer thrust a violently wriggling sack at Mark. "Get rid of it for me, will you? The wife can't stand it," he said. "Put it on the account."

Mark sighed. He hated to destroy life, but it was a part of his job that he had to accept. Marny became curious about the sack squirming about on the back seat. She leant over and gingerly untied the string, and instantly a ball of fluffy fury leapt on to the top of the seat and hissed defiance at her. Mark saw the kitten in the driving mirror, its teeth bared and claws extended, its striped fur up on its back and the wisp of a tail swishing in anger.

"Not much to recommend *him.*"

"No. He's a real ugly duckling," laughed Marny.

The station wagon drew up at the Mann house, but Mark refused to come in for a cup of tea.

"I'm off. Put the cat back in the bag."

"No, I'll keep him."

"You're crazy, Marny. It's half-wild."

"I know," she agreed. "But he needs a friend."

"It's O.K. by me. I only hope that your parents won't mind. What's his name?"

"Why, Ugly Duckling of course!" And Marny scooped her kitten back into the bag and ran inside. Her parents were so pleased to see their daughter cheerful again that they accepted Ugly Duckling without any fuss. Only Whisky was annoyed, and showed his feelings by going under the kitchen table and staying there.

"I'll call you Whisky Sour if you don't cheer up," his mistress told him sternly. Whisky ignored her. The kitten was locked in the bathroom for a cooling off period, and the family settled down for tea.

Sunday morning was a clear, bright day with a nip in the air—the sort of day that made you want to gallop over the hills. Marny thought about something Mark had said yesterday while they were driving back from the Roberts place. "You can't grieve for Sure Smile forever, Marny. Everyone has to carry on after disappointments." He was right. She couldn't stop riding because she had lost one horse. But in spite of her brave words to her father the day before, she needed all her courage to visit Alex Shooter's riding school. Last time had been the week before the show, when she and Alex had had a friendly jumping competition. Now she would have to arrive on her bicycle, and Sure Smile was....Marny brushed the tears from her eyes and ran into the kitchen. Trudy smiled at her lovingly when Marny told her where she was going.

"Have a lovely time and don't hurry home. I'll have dinner waiting for you."

Instead of riding round the bridle path leading to the indoor school, Marny cycled through the main gate and under Alex's large wrought-iron sign: SHOOTER'S RIDING ACADEMY. Prof. A. Shooter, M.E.F.A., H.M. (U.S.A.). The grazing paddocks on either side of the drive were empty, for Alex's horses had a full working day on a Sunday. The guard rails were freshly painted white and the iron gates green. Everything looked neat and prosperous. Marny wished that her old jodhpurs were smarter and her boots newer. She reached the indoor school and quietly opened the sliding doors leading to the *manège,* trying to slip in unnoticed.

"Hi, there, Marny. Great to have you back," came a shout from Mrs. Rowbotham, who always noticed everything. Alex was giving a lunge lesson. One girl had just finished, and Mrs. Rowbotham's turn was next. Winston, a good-humoured bay hunter, stood patiently in the circle while Mrs. Rowbotham prepared to mount, and Marny and the other pupils tried not to look at one another and laugh. Mrs. Rowbotham had been taking regular lessons for two years. Perhaps if she were not such a good client Alex would have been kind enough to tell her that her problem was her bottom. It was too large for a standard 43-centimetre saddle tree.

The plump woman gave Winston a great friendly thwack, and he jumped as her heavy hand descended on his rump. Mrs. Rowbotham was tastefully attired in tight blue jeans, an orange shirt, and a very small jockey cap. Her round face beamed happily at everyone. Alex gave her a leg up. Not expecting her enthusiasm to lend her such energy, he gave a powerful heave, sending the good lady soaring over Winston's broad back. She made desperate attempts to cling to the saddle as she slowly sank to the sand like a pricked balloon. The pupils immediately began various complicated manoeuvres to prevent themselves from laughing. Barry and Blair tried sneezing. Marny fiddled with her boots, and Alice stuffed a handkerchief into her mouth. Alex pursed his lips and began twirling the end of the whip. Relief came when Mrs. Rowbotham started to laugh herself and they could join in openly.

"Guess I'd better try again." This time she managed to mount successfully, and Winston began to slow walkmarch as Alex held the lunge-rein and the long whip. Mrs. Rowbotham described her circles, uttering little clicking sounds like a rusty typewriter. Barry gave Blair a nudge, and Blair came over to where Marny was standing.

"Marny."

"Yes?"

"You've not been around much lately."

"No, I've been busy." She hoped desperately that he wouldn't mention Sure Smile. That wound was too raw to be touched.

"Marny, we've got a 'do' on tonight at my place. Candy's coming. Will you?"

Mrs. Rowbotham's lesson was speeding up.

"You aren't going anywhere tonight, are you?"

"No."

"Then say you'll come."

Marny couldn't think of a polite refusal. Blair looked at her appealingly.

"Thanks, Blair. I'd love to."

She turned her back on him to watch Winston, who was slowing down again. Without warning, Alex cracked his whip, and the lash flashed upwards before plunging down into Winston's warm brown hide. The gelding leapt in pain and grunted—an involuntary noise as the air hissed through his larynx. "That's better! Canter on, you lazy devil!"

Mrs. Rowbotham wobbled dangerously as Winston broke into an unbalanced canter. Blair and Barry stood unconcerned as Alex flicked his whip about. They were kind boys, fond of animals, but Alex had taught them all they knew and they had learned no better. Marny had to watch in silence. She too had been taught at the Shooter Academy, but her natural sensitivity made her doubt the Shooter methods. However, she had no authority to back her up and Alex's reputation in the district stood high. He always carried a whip and used it regularly on his animals.

Winston's canter slowed to a trot as Alex called out, "Sitting trot, please. Sitting. *Sitting.*"

"I *am* sitting," came the plaintive reply as Mrs. Rowbotham bounced irregularly in the saddle. Winston halted and his rider scrambled off.

"Thanks, old boy," she said, thumping the gelding affectionately. "Well, I guess there's still a lot more to learn." She handed round a bag of sweets and settled down to watch the others.

It was Barry's turn next. A popular boy, he was tall and athletic, with a tendency to acne. With an easy leap, he vaulted on to the saddle.

"Jolly good," cheered Mrs. Rowbotham. Barry gave a boxer's salute and began his lesson.

"Hasn't Barry improved?" Marny commented to Alice. She had noted how much deeper he was sitting in the saddle.

"I suppose so," said Alice, grudgingly, as Barry returned sweating and panting from his exertions on the lunge without stirrups or reins. Alex had worked him hard and made him perform several exhausting exercises.

"Boy!" he gasped. "Do I *pay* to do this? I must be mad. How'd I do, Marny?"

"You're improving fast."

Alice interrupted. She expected her father's young clients to be *her* admirers; and indeed many of them did come to the school after seeing her perform on Mirabelle at shows. Alice managed to hide her nasty side from most people.

"You can try Mirabelle next week," she told Barry.

"Gosh, thanks, Alice. You're a sport."

Blair's turn was next. He wasn't as skilled as Barry, being tubby and unable to grip with his knees. Although he tried hard, he always looked uncomfortable. He could never understand why he found football so easy and riding so difficult. Alex gave him a much less severe workout, after which he dismounted and pretended to stagger back to the group.

"Your turn, Alice and Marny." Alex called out.

"How about a fresh horse?" Marny suggested quietly.

Winston was obviously tired after four pupils had bounced in varying degrees of hardness up and down on his back. Although Alex's horses looked well fed, he cut down on their oat ration and substituted bran and hay to prevent them growing too lively for his clients. In addition, to save money on his feed bills, he used inferior quality food grains. Few people were expert enough to realise that the seemingly fat horses lacked gaiety in their stride and keenness for their work. But Alex took Marny's suggestion for a fresh horse at its face value.

"Good idea. Go and bring in Sultan."

Marny went off to fetch the horse, and Blair followed her.

"I have to leave the lesson now," he told her. "But you are coming tonight, aren't you? It's very important to me."

She nodded, and Blair said, "Good girl. See you later."

Sultan was standing quietly in his stall. He had been a well-known jumper in his day and had carried Alex to many victories. Now he was semi-retired. Marny led him into the *manège*, stopping on the way to clean out his hooves. He had been brushed that morning but his feet had been left full of grit and tiny stones. Marny helped Alex swap saddles over and Alice led the sweating Winston back to his stall.

Alex gave Marny and Alice ten minutes each on the lunge. He observed each girl in turn. He saw how easily Marny sank into the saddle, her long legs clinging effortlessly to the horse's sides. Alice looked more elegant, and her seat was superficially correct, but she lacked that inner harmony which characterised all Marny's actions on horseback.

"Funny," thought Alex. "That awkward Mann girl loses any trace of clumsiness once she's up on a horse. She looks as if she's known how to ride all her life, but Alice looks as if she's learnt it all." But he stored his observations away for a rainy day, and said nothing to the girls.

"Come on now, Marny. Touch your left toe with your right hand."

Marny's bottom rose in the air in her efforts to reach her foot.

"Not supple enough yet, I see. A daily ride for you for some time. Tell the doctor that's *my* prescription."

"Thanks, I will."

"No charge, of course. You can pay your way with stable chores," he said grandly.

"I'll try," said Marny, giving him a shy smile. When she smiled her rather angular face altered and she became almost beautiful. Alice frowned.

When the lesson was over, the two girls had the job of putting Sultan away and closing up the *manège*.

"Are you by any chance going to Blair's tonight?" Alice asked, all sweetness.

"Yes, I am. Aren't you going?" Marny replied naively, not realising that Blair hadn't asked Alice. "Why don't we go together? Come and pick me up. My house is on the way."

Alice had got the invitation she wanted. She was delighted. "See you tonight then. "Bye. You know, I really was sorry about Sure Smile."

Marny pretended not to hear this last tactless remark and went home quickly.

Trudy was pleased that Marny had at last accepted an invitation to go out in the evening. "Such a good class of youngsters you meet at Mr. Shooter's," she gushed.

"Oh, *please* stop, Mum. I don't really want to go anyway."

She ran into her room to change. Although Trudy would have liked her to wear a pretty frock, she only brushed her long straggly hair and put on clean jeans and a shirt. But in a shirt the same shade of green as her eyes, and with her normally pale face delicately flushed, she looked lovely. Alice, arriving to fetch her, looked overdressed beside her, wearing black pants, a low-cut blouse, and loads of eye make-up.

"It's so kind of you to take Marianne out with you, Alice."

"That's all right, Mrs. Mann," said Alice airily, not bothering to tell Trudy who was taking whom.

"Bye Mum. I won't be late." Marny wished she did not have to go at all: she was dreading the evening ahead. If Alice had not been there she would probably have made up some excuse and stayed at home. The two girls walked to Blair's house, only a few blocks away.

"You see, Sigi," Trudy said, when they were alone again. "Now *Liebchen* is growing up and going to parties like other young ladies. Not so much horses in future."

"Humph," replied Sigi. He knew Marny better than her mother. He doubted very much if a single party would alter Marny's lifelong love for horses.

Chapter 6

At Blair's house, Marny and Alice found the furniture pushed
back against the wall, carpets rolled up, and music blaring from
the record player.

"Hiya. Glad you made it." Blair pulled Marny out on to
the impromptu dance floor, and Alice was swept up into a
group of her father's pupils. Blair whispered something in
Marny's ear.

"I can't hear you. The music's too loud."

"I said you look beaut," he bellowed. Everyone laughed and
Marny blushed. She wished Blair wouldn't clutch her so tightly—
nobody else danced like that. She looked for Candida but saw
that she was sitting on the sofa with Barry. At last the record
ended, but still Blair kept hold of her.

"Come on everyone!" he called. "Supper!"

Blair's mother had provided a scrumptious meal, set it out,
and then tactfully gone with her husband to the pictures. There
were cold chicken, lamb, and turkey, bowls of salads, and a fruit
punch, Marny found that being shy didn't stop her being
hungry.

"Good girl," Blair said, pleased to see her heaped plate.
"I can't stand these chicken feeders. Have some more punch."
The attention made Marny feel dizzy, and she couldn't seem to
get Blair's arm off her waist. Candida and Barry left their sofa
and came to sit with them, both carrying loaded plates.

"Hiya. Tried the cheesecake yet? Fantastic!"

"You do look pretty, Marny," said Barry. She did. The candle-light flattered her pale skin and made her hair shine like gold coins.

At this point they were joined by a young man whom Marny had never seen before.

"Hiya, Pete. Great to see you!" Blair pumped the tall boy's hand, and the stranger winced. He was blonde with finely-cut features and very clear skin, and seemed to be a few years older than most of the others. Marny noticed that he limped slightly.

"Sorry I'm late. Couldn't get the car to start."

"Never mind. Meet Marny."

"Hello."

"Hello," said the newcomer. "I'm Peter Cooke-Finch. I believe we haven't met before."

"No, we haven't." Marny could think of nothing else to say. They stood in silence. Usually Marny had to stoop down to the local boys to talk to them, but Peter was a lot taller than she was. Her green eyes looked up into his dark-grey ones and she felt awkward.

"Excuse me, see you later." He left them and joined Alice's group. Alice seemed pleased to see him.

"Seems stuck up, doesn't he?" Blair commented. "He's in the same year as Barry."

"What's he studying, Barry?" asked Candida.

"Same as me," replied Barry. "Agricultural Economics. He won't need to get a job, though. His dad's bought up the Calder place. They're loaded."

"The sort of rich boy Alice likes," said Blair. "What's she doing here, anyway? I didn't ask her."

"Oh," said Marny, blushing. "I brought her." So *that* explained Alice's friendliness during the lunge lesson. She gazed over at Alice, now chatting vivaciously with Peter Cooke-Finch, and felt an inexplicable twinge of envy. Alice always seemed to come out on top, no matter what she did. Peter was bending down to hear what she was saying, and Alice, perfectly aware that Peter was the best-looking boy in the room, was pressing her advantage by flirting outrageously.

Blair interrupted her reverie. "Oh, Marny," he said in a squeaky falsetto, "you mustn't let yourself be carried off by the rich stranger. Give us local lads a chance!"

"Blair, stop teasing her," said Candida. "Anyway, I don't think the Cooke-Finch boy is stuck-up. He's just shy and trying not to show it."

"We'll have to make a match, then," said Blair, still clowning. "Shy Peter and shy Marny. They must be made for each other!'

Marny's embarrassment turned to irritation. "I have to go home now, Blair. I've got school tomorrow."

"We've all got classes too. Don't rush off."

"I told you to stop teasing her," warned Candida.

"It's not that at all. Please let go of me, Blair," Marny was already struggling into her parka. "Thanks for the party."

"*Please* don't go, Marny. Hang on a bit and I'll walk you home."

"Don't bother," she called, already on her way to the door. "It's not far." And before Blair could argue any more, she had gone.

"Whew, I'm glad to be home!" Her room had never looked more welcoming. The walls were covered with photos of Sunshine and Sure Smile and horsey pictures cut out of magazines. Beside the bed was a warm sheepskin rug which a farmer had given her for catching his escaped bull. It was blessedly quiet. "I don't think nightlife is meant for me, Whisky." He agreed by wagging his rump. She took his tartan coat down from the shelf and prepared to rug him up for the night. Although Trudy told her that Corgis are bred to withstand Welsh winters, Marny said that if *she* felt cold in the Armidale winter, then Whisky would too. So Whisky wore his coat at night and slept curled up on her bed. In the morning, though, he refused to go out until it had been taken off. Perhaps he was afraid his hunting mates would laugh at him—particularly Taffy, Candida's Labrador. These two were great friends. The short-legged Corgi could scrabble right down into the rabbit holes and the long-legged Labrador could outrun any small animal, yet their combined efforts never resulted in a kill. Marny thought they were too squeamish to kill anything. It was the chase that mattered.

Marny woke up much later than usual. Trudy was calling happily down the hallway: "You'll miss the school bus! Hurry!" She liked waking up her daughter after an evening's party: it reminded her of her own youth.

"Oh, *Liebchen*," she said now. "If you knew how gay I used to be at your age! My mother couldn't keep me in dancing slippers."

"Sorry, Mum. Can't stop now. Tell me about it tonight." Marny grabbed a piece of toast and ran for the bus stop, arriving just as the battered green school bus drew up with a rattle.

"I'm sure this thing's going to fall apart on us one day," said one of the students.

"Let's hope it's a Monday," said Marny. "I hate them."

"Me too!" came a chorus of voices. But there was no such luck today: with a determined report from the exhaust, the bus roared off towards the centre of town.

Marny quickly settled down to her lessons and forgot Monday blues. She was immersed in her maths when Candida interrupted her with: "Come on, swot. It's lunchtime."

The two girls ate their sandwiches in a secluded corner of the school grounds and re-lived every detail of last night's party.

"Aren't you glad you've started to go out again?" Candida asked her friend.

"Not really. I mean, I like seeing everyone, and dancing's fun, but the whole thing just makes me shyer."

"What did you think of that new boy?"

"Which one?"

"There *was* only one—Peter. Peter Cooke-Finch. He liked you."

"Candy, don't be so romantic! He didn't say two words to me before he went off to Alice's lot. He's *her* type, not mine." Honestly, she thought to herself, I do wish everyone would stop talking about Peter Cooke-Finch. I'm getting sick of the sound of his name.

Candida offered her a meat-loaf sandwich in exchange for one of hers. She thought Marny's sandwiches had very exotic fillings. "I wish my mum cooked like yours," she commented, licking her lips. Then she looked serious for a moment. "It would be lovely if you were going out with someone too," she said

38

wistfully. "We've always shared everything and done things together, and now it just won't be the same."

"But why ever not? I'm still me, and you're still you. I don't need a boyfriend to prove anything. And in any case it's not as if you and Barry are engaged! We can still do things together."

Candida looked rather abashed. "Of course we can! I just meant....Oh, I don't know. It's just more *complete*, somehow." She laughed. "You know, Marny, I really think you care more about animals than people!"

"You might be right," said Marny, snapping her lunchbox shut. "Come on, there's the bell."

Afternoon school passed quickly, and soon the three-thirty bell rang, releasing some hundred girls and boys to freedom. The bus was waiting outside to pick them up. Candida was dropped off first, and Marny watched her reach down into the prickly bush where she hid her bike each morning. "I hope she doesn't get back one day and find someone's pinched it," thought Marny, laughing as her friend triumphantly retrieved her property.

Candida pedalled away as fast as the old pushbike would allow, waving her hand cheerfully at the departing bus. She hurried because her little brother, Micky, wasn't well. If she reached home early enough she would be able to baby-sit for her mother, and Janey could go into town to do the weekly shopping. Marny was among the last students to get off the bus. After she had alighted she turned for home, walking alongside the railway siding. The stockyards were filled with horses.

"Poor creatures," thought Marny. A batch of these unwanted horses arrived several times each year in the Armidale stockyards to rest overnight before being sent 586 kilometres to the Sydney slaughter houses. They were all sorts: broken-down hacks, ancient ridingschool ponies, worn-out stock horses. What a cruel end to a lifetime of service!

As Marny was passing the yard with its characteristic smell of creosote, she heard a loud crack of splintering wood. A big raw-boned chestnut had burst out from a back stall into the yard. Men shouted as he cleared the sides of the 180-centimetre post-and-rail fence. It was an incredible leap. He galloped past, a broken rope dangling from his neck, his eyes rolling in terror.

Chapter 7

Marny did not stop to consider what she was doing. As the big horse thundered past, she grabbed hold of the free end of the rope and hung on. Her slight weight did not slow down the tearaway. She was dragged along like a skiff in the wake of a destroyer. Traffic halted and hooted as the pair veered across the road, for the horse had no idea where he was going. Somehow Marny kept hold of the rope. Her hands were protected a little by her gloves, or she could not have done it. But unless the terrified animal halted soon, she would have to let go. Her hands were numb and her arms felt as though they were being wrenched from their sockets. If she did let go, she was sure the horse would be killed when he met the rush of homeward-bound cars coming from the centre of town.

Then, gradually, she realised that she was not alone: someone had caught hold of the other end of the neckrope. It was Peter Cooke-Finch. Together they braced themselves against the weight of the terrified animal. For the first time, the big horse began to listen to Marny's voice as she coaxed and pleaded, and finally he slowed down and stood still, eyes dilated, nostrils flared, his whole body trembling. His chestnut coat was streaked dark brown with sweat. Marny approached him slowly, without taking her gaze from his or stopping her soft crooning. He sniffed at her outstretched hand, then his ears shot back and his teeth flashed. Marny had seen the warning signs and pulled her hand

back in time. All the chestnut was left with were a few shreds of school blazer.

"Careful, Marny," warned Peter. He moved protectively behind her, ready to take over if the horse turned savage again. Marny knew that without his help the horse would probably have been run over, but all she said was: "Please. It's best if you don't interfere." Peter said nothing, but went on helping.

They constructed a makeshift halter out of the frayed neck-rope. It fitted low over his nose. He continued to pull against it, his eyes full of hatred, but he was as exhausted as they were. As the three of them continued up the road, Marny noticed again that Peter limped slightly. In silent agreement they were leading the horse *away* from the railway yards.

Finally Peter broke the silence. "Where to, Marny?" She did not answer, and he saw that she was in a state of shock. He had heard what had happened to Sure Smile, and he supposed the danger that the big horse could have been run over had brought back painful memories. He thought he heard her muttering to herself, "I won't let them take *him* away."

At last Peter was able to get a proper look at the animal. He was a big chestnut gelding, well over sixteen hands, with the small, beautiful head of a Thoroughbred and a mean look in his eye.

"He's vicious," said Peter. But Marny continued to ignore his remarks.

Their pace was slow, and in a few minutes two men from the railway yards had caught up with them. They were accompanied by a policeman. The instant he saw the men, the chestnut reared, striking out with his forefeet as a fighting stallion does. Neither Peter nor Marny had anticipated this reaction, and the gelding tore the rope out of their hands and reared again and again. There were screams from pedestrians, and car drivers tooted their horns and shouted, "Control that horse!" The railway men, terrified, were cowering away, not knowing what to do. "Come here, you fools!" Peter yelled at them.

Then Marny stumbled into the path of the flailing hooves. Peter darted in front of her and, grasping the halter, tightened it over the horse's nostrils, cutting off his air supply. The horse, gasping for breath, quietened.

"God, Marny! You might have been killed!"

"C'mon, hand over that fireball," said one of the railway workers, aggressive now the danger was past.

"Who legally owns this animal?" demanded the policeman. By now a small crowd had gathered. Everyone began talking at once. Marny, reduced to semi-hysteria, cried out, "You can't have him!" But the chestnut stood aloof. He no longer cared what fate had in store for him. Whatever it was, he was prepared to meet it with his own kind of courage and his hatred for all men.

Peter ended the argument by producing a cheque book. "All right, then. I shall buy the animal. What's he worth?" Although this was highly irregular, the railway men were glad to get rid of the vicious horse.

"He's a killer," muttered one of them darkly. "Silly young fool, letting that lass anywhere near him!" But the other man, who was in charge, was very satisfied with the large tip Peter added to the price he had quoted. After he had written out a receipt on

43

the back of an old envelope, the two railwaymen went away whistling.

"Keep that animal under control,"said the policeman.

"Certainly, officer. We will," said Peter, confidently.

So Marny and Peter were left holding the horse, who seemed to be only temporarily quietened. The problem was: what to do next?

"Let's take him to Alex Shooter's, Marny," suggested Peter. "You can't manage him alone."

"If you like," came the reply. "He's your horse, isn't he?"

"No, of course he isn't. I bought him because you said you couldn't give him up. He's *your* horse."

"But Peter, *you* paid for him!"

"Pay me back whenever you like. It was only a hundred dollars."

"*Only?* I haven't got the money."

"Don't worry about it, then. There's no hurry."

"Thanks," Marny said confusedly. Her pleasure was mingled with embarrassment, for she was now under an obligation to this boy she hardly knew.

If Alex was surprised to see them bring the big horse into his yard, he did not show it. His practised eye recognised the gelding's quality at once, but all he said was, "That horse is done in. Put him in the end box and bed him down." As Peter led his new charge into the box, the animal started lashing out again with hooves and teeth. Peter managed to get out unhurt, and the chestnut continued to kick wildly at the boards.

"Looks like a killer," said Alex. "Where'd you get him?"

"He's Marny's. We just bought him off the railway yard. He was due for the slaughter house."

"Has he any papers with him?"

"Nope. Absolutely no credentials."

Marny broke in: "He's mine! I mean to keep him!"

Alex began to laugh. "He'll never be any use to *you*, Marny. He's too big and mean. *I* might be able to handle him, though. He looks to have a useful leap in him. Don't you think?" He turned again to Peter.

"What are you asking *him* for?" Marny cried out. "He's *my* horse! Peter lent me the money to buy this one, but that's *all!*" And she suddenly burst into tears.

44

"Whatever's up with you?" Alex was amazed at Marny's outburst.

Peter bit his lip and turned away. "I'm off," he told Alex. They watched him stride down the path, limping more noticeably now that he was tired.

"Come on, Marny girl. Stop your snivels. It's not like you," Alex said, not unkindly. He fed and watered the new arrival, noting with approval the long strides the horse took as he restlessly paced up and down his box.

Marny got up from the hay bale she had been sitting on, feeling confused and light-headed. Everyone said Peter Cooke-Finch was stuck-up and Alice Shooter had stated that he'd had nothing to do with horses. Yet he had handled the wild chestnut with real authority. It was a mystery. Nor did she understand why Peter made her angry just because he was so calm. She was behaving most unlike her normal self

"Mr. Shooter, thank you for all your help. I'll come tomorrow and see how he's getting on."

"Now, don't worry about anything," Alex said, his small eyes gleaming greedily. "I'll see to the horse." It was not every day that a Thoroughbred of that quality arrived in a riding school, and Alex meant to get hold of the animal for himself if he possibly could.

Marny began the long walk home, her tired brain full of confused memories of the rearing horse, of Peter, and of Alex's overfriendliness.

She arrived home late, to find that her parents had been anxiously wondering where she was. How was she ever going to tell her father that she had acquired a new horse—let alone such a horse as this savage fireball?

Chapter 8

Next day, Marny waited until the end of breakfast before telling her parents about the new horse. As soon as she'd left the house to catch the school bus Sigi said: "I thought you said all this horse business was over. Going to parties hasn't made any difference."

"Don't blame me," Trudy replied. "*My* father wasn't a Hungarian cowboy. Yours was."

"What's that got to do with it?"

"Horses are in her blood."

"Nonsense! That's not scientific."

"Well, scientific or not," said practical Trudy, "what are we going to do? She's rushed off to school late. She's forgotten her maths book. And now we'll have the old problem all over again." She sighed. "Just when I was so sure she was starting to have boyfriends and go out like other young ladies."

"I blame Mark," said Sigi. "He started off by giving her Sunshine. Sure Smile was worse, and this one will be the worst of all. You mark my words."

She gloomily agreed with him, and they sat in silence until their coffee grew cold and Trudy had to make a fresh pot.

When Marny returned from school, she escaped quickly to her room, saying she had a lot of homework to do. Even her pets sensed her disgrace and skulked about the house. Ugly Duckling decided to move out to the empty stable and came indoors only to eat.

"Am I expected to pay for this foolishness of yours?" Sigi asked at tea.

"Please, Dad. It's only a hundred dollars. I'll pay you back."

"I shall pay Mr. Cooke-Finch this money, Marianne. I regard it as a debt of honour."

Marny rushed up to kiss her father, but he stopped her. "No, I do *not* wish your thanks, Marianne. I said 'debt of honour.' I did not say I approved."

"Oh, Mum—can't you help me explain?"

"But Marny, darling," Trudy said sadly, torn between the two of them. "We thought all this horse business was over. Now that Sure Smile....And you were getting on so well at the stables. Such a nice class of youngsters you were meeting there. Now all you'll do will be to fight with this horse, and he sounds so wild...."

"Oh, you don't understand, either of you!...." Marny ran down the hall and they heard her bedroom door slam shut.

That weekend, when everyone in the Mann household was upset about the horse, Peter went home to visit his father. They toured the property, and Charles Cooke-Finch showed his son the latest improvements.

"It's great, Dad. I can't wait to finish my degree and come out here with you. I've got so many new ideas."

"I know you're anxious to get started. I'm lucky to have a son who wants to follow in my footsteps."

Peter laughed. "Especially when you change direction. All this is a bit different from Surrey."

"Yes. But you didn't want to stay in England any more than I did, after your mother died. And that awful business with Cantrece."

"What happened to Cantrece was my fault, Dad. She wasn't fit enough for the point-to-point. I'll never forgive myself for entering her—and killing her."

" 'Never' is a long time, son. You should stop blaming yourself. You were too upset over your mother's death to use good judgement, and you were very young." Charles gazed towards the wide, shimmering horizon. "We're in a new country now, and we've both been given a fresh start. Not many people are so lucky."

48

"Of course, you're right, Dad. But I don't want another horse. That's certain."

"You've time on your side, Peter. Your leg will get better....Speaking of horses, have you heard from the Mann girl?"

"No, I haven't. A cheque arrived yesterday from her father, to pay for that horse. Not even a note from her. I think she's peculiar."

"I don't," said Charles. "I like the girl."

"I didn't know you'd met her."

"I went to town last week to consult her father about my rheumatism. They invited me for coffee, and Marianne came in briefly."

"Did she speak to you?"

"Hardly a word. But I think I understand her. She's shy, and devilish proud, and she must hate the idea of owing you anything."

"You're probably right again, as usual. I still feel annoyed— nearly getting run over helping her, and then getting precious little thanks."

"Girls can be like that, Peter, you'll find. Especially good ones like Marianne Mann. I'd help her tame her wild horse if she asked me."

"She won't ask *me* for anything," Peter said. "I don't think she likes me very much."

"We can only wait and see." Changing the topic, they talked about the farm again. During lunch, Peter noticed that his father was smiling in an oddly selfsatisfied way. When he left to return to university, he said, "If I see her I won't ask about the horse. If she wants anything she'll have to come to me."

"Of course," said Charles, with the same smile.

Every day Marny went to Alex Shooter's, but the big horse was not settling down. Finally Alex said, "See here, Marny. I can't allow you to go in to him. He's too savage, and I can't risk a major accident on my place."

"I do understand, but can't I try?" Marny took the bucket of water from Alex and approached the box confidently. As she started to unlatch the door, a chestnut head swooped out with the speed of a snake striking, and she narrowly avoided the flashing teeth.

49

"Is that enough proof?" demanded Alex. He raised his whip and cracked it across the horse's muzzle. The chestnut backed sullenly into a corner of the box, his eyes rolling until the whites showed. Alex put down the water bucket. As he turned his back, the horse wheeled and lashed out with his hind legs.

"Try that again, would you?" Alex whipped the chestnut over his back and shoulders.

"Oh, please stop!" cried Marny.

"It's no use being soft with a horse like that, my girl. All he understands is brute force. I told you before: he's vicious."

"I wish you'd let me try my way," she pleaded.

"Look here, Marny. While that horse is here, he's treated *my* way. You can always take him away."

Marny couldn't argue. He was right. It *was* his stable; and Sigi wouldn't let her bring the horse home.

That night, while Marny was asleep, Alex Shooter came to see Sigi.

"I've decided to make you a handsome offer for that savage beast," he said, grandly. "I know what you paid and I'll add three tens—give you a hundred and thirty dollars. How's that for an offer?"

Sigi shook his head. "That horse does not belong to me, Mr. Shooter. I paid the money, but he belongs to Marianne. Much as I should be delighted to accommodate you, you must address yourself to her."

"Come off it, Doctor. She's your kid, isn't she? If I told my Alice I was going to get rid of Mirabelle, she'd have no choice in the matter."

"Perhaps. But Marianne is not Alice and I am not you. So I will have to bid you good evening."

Alex was forced to leave, muttering as he went, "Fancy turning down a hundred and thirty dollars for that ratbag. Some folks don't know when they're lucky."

Although her parents did not tell Marny about Alex's offer, the incident seemed to clear the air. The house grew less gloomy, and Whisky stopped skulking under the furniture. Only Ugly Duckling continued to prefer the stable.

50

April passed, bringing the cold winds of May. Whisky was glad of his tartan coat on these chilly mornings, and Marny had to struggle to get up for school. Every evening and weekend she went to the riding stables. Her big chestnut gelding remained nameless and was growing thinner and more ill-kempt. Alex was starving him into submission.

Marny had no one to turn to for help or advice. Mark Thomas had taken Melissa for a long holiday in Greece, and she had heard no more from the Cooke-Finches. Blair pestered her to go out with him, but she made excuses every time he telephoned her.

One Saturday she went to the Thomas home to stay the night. The two girls lay awake in Candida's pretty room and talked for hours.

"I don't know what to do, Candy," confessed Marny. "Alex says the horse is improving, but I'm sure he isn't. His hooves are nearly splitting, and all his ribs stick out."

"He can't be as wild as he was, can he?" Candida had only seen the horse once.

"That's just the problem. Sometimes I think he recognises me. Then if Alex comes anywhere in sight he goes wild and Alex beats him. I don't know what to do."

"I don't either," sighed her friend.

"But it's not your problem."

"Of course it's my problem. When he goes back to university and all those girls start chasing him ...."

"Goes back to university? Are you crazy? How can a horse go to uni?"

"Oh, Marny!" Candida broke into peals of laughter. "I'm talking about *Barry*. He's such a Casanova."

"Casanova? What a lovely name! Candy, I've got it! We'll call him Casanova!"

"Who? Barry or your horse?"

"My horse, stupid. If he's got a name, maybe he'll be happier."

"Well, it is a nice name, and it will suit him one day."

"Who? Barry or my horse?"

"Your horse, stupid." At that, the girls laughed so loudly that Susy, Candida's younger sister, banged on the wall.

51

"I don't think you should worry about Barry. Anyone can see he's keen on you."

"Marny, you are a comfort. I hope it'll be your turn next."

"Not a chance," said Marny. "I have Casanova to worry about. I don't want a boyfriend as well."

One winter's evening a few weeks later, Marny had just begun her homework when her mother called her to the telephone. It was Alice. She sounded frightened.

"Marny, can you get here straight away?"

"What's wrong?"

"It's Dad. He's in the *manège* with your horse. They've been there for over an hour, and there are horrible noises coming out. I'm scared. I won't go in. Will you come?"

"I'm coming." Marny felt so afraid she couldn't breathe properly. Without telling her parents where she was going, she ran to get her bicycle. She covered the three kilometres to the riding school in ten minutes. The stable yard was in darkness except for lights coming from the *manège*. She slid the heavy doors apart silently, and went inside.

Four big arc-lights set in the corner of the school's ceiling harshly lit up the battle between the man and the horse. Casanova was standing at the end of the lunge-line. The side-reins were tightly fastened, preventing him from stretching his neck out. Alex stood in the centre, holding his lungeing-whip. Marny saw that he had fixed extra thongs at the end so that it was no longer an instrument of correction and training but one of torture. Alex was in a furious rage. A half-finished whisky bottle was lying at his feet.

"He must be drunk," Marny thought with horror. He was trying to drive Casanova into a trot, and the animal's flanks were covered in a foaming white sweat. As Marny crept closer to the circle, she saw drops of blood on his neck. The terrible whip had split open his right ear all along its side, exposing the raw flesh.

"Trot on, you brute," Alex shouted. Casanova broke into a tired trot, but Alex did not let up the pressure. He gave the lunge-rein a savage jerk, causing the horse to throw up his head with pain. The moment the head was raised, Alex flicked the whip. The lash caught one eye, which closed immediately.

52

But Alex had gone too far. The horse gathered his failing strength and struck out at his tormentor. Rearing with such force that he broke the side-reins, he charged blindly forward and caught the man in the chest, bringing him to his knees. As he swung round again to attack with bared teeth, Alex beat him off, wielding the whip-butt like a sword. The horse charged again. Marny shut her eyes. When she opened them, Alex had seized a jumping-pole and swung it at the horse's forelegs. It hit the chestnut's knee with a sickening crunch. Casanova paused—just long enough to allow Alex to run like a scalded cat for the exit. The man's luck held. Marny had not quite shut the sliding doors and he reached them a few metres before the horse did. He slipped through to safety and clanged the doors behind him. He had not even seen Marny.

When his tormentor had gone, Casanova pawed the ground and neighed triumphantly. Then his head. drooped and he stood still, leaving the lunge-line and broken reins trailing—not a vicious attacker, but a weary animal, bruised, beaten, and exhausted. One foreleg trembled uncontrollably. Trembling herself, Marny approached him. Casanova remained quiet and allowed her to remove the tack and throw it to the ground. Then she slid her leather belt out of her jeans and hooped it around the tired neck.

Slowly she led the horse out of the *manège*. They walked as though in a dream, with mist and darkness all around them. Marny expected to hear shouts from the Shooter house, but there was no sound except for the quiet clop of Casanova's un-shod hooves. From time to time a shudder ran through the horse's tired body. Marny soothed him with gentle words. "Come on, boy," she murmured. "We're going home." Tears ran un-heeded down her cheeks as she felt the whip-marks along his sides. "I'm sorry. I'm sorry," she kept whispering.

She put him in Sure Smile's old stable. He stood there rest-ing his injured foreleg, too weary to eat or drink.

"Marny, Marny, what have you done?" Trudy scolded. "I saw the lights in the yard. Where have you been?"

"Oh, Mum!" Marny collapsed, sobbing, in her mother's arms. "I'm sorry. I couldn't help it. Alex beat him. Casanova tried to kill him. I saw everything, Mum. It was horrible."

Trudy soothed her. "Never mind, it's over. It's over. You mustn't think about it."

"But it was my fault. I shouldn't have left him there. Can I stay with him tonight? Please, Mum."

And Trudy surprised herself by saying instantly: "Of course." She felt certain that the big horse would not harm her daughter. Marny fetched her sleeping-bag, took it down to the stable, and laid it out on the straw. The horse was already down. Within minutes, Marny was asleep too.

Chapter 9

First thing next morning, Alex Shooter arrived at the Mann house. He was unshaven and his eyes were bloodshot. Trudy let him in.

"Morning," he said, looking around suspiciously to see if Marny was near by. "I've come about the horse."

"Which horse?" Alex's tone annoyed Sigi.

"That raw-boned monstrosity your daughter calls Casanova. How did Marny get hold of it?"

"I suppose she found him wandering loose around the stables last night and brought him home."

"That horse tried to kill me. It's a killer. The only place for it is in the railway yards on the way to the knackers, where you found it. I wouldn't let my daughter near it."

Alex's attitude was calculated to annoy Sigi, who hated being told what to do. "I suggest we go down to the stables to hear what Marny has to say," he said urbanely.

"No thank *you.*" Alex had no intention of meeting either the girl or the horse face to face. Not after last night. He was still uncertain whether or not Marny had seen the battle.

"I've done my duty, Doctor Mann. I've warned you. If you won't listen, I'll say good morning. I've a busy day ahead of me at the stables and I've wasted too much time already on that mad horse. It should be destroyed, like I've told you. No thanks, Mrs. Mann. No coffee." The aroma of coffee followed his retreating back.

"What an unpleasant man!" Sigi commented cheerfully. "We made a real mistake letting Marny spend so much time at his establishment. Well, I'm going to the stable to see this horse."

Trudy was left holding the coffee pot, too astonished to speak. "I'll never understand that man I married," she thought, feeding cake to Whisky, who wagged his tail sympathetically, "but I love him all the same."

Sigi marched energetically down the narrow path leading to the stable yard. He was short and balding and growing stout, but he swung his arms in time to a martial tune he was humming. Marny and the horse were not in sight. He peered through the open stable door. Immediately a chestnut head whipped out and Sigi leapt back, barely evading the snap of the jaws. Marny heard the commotion and rushed out from the tack room.

"Oh Dad! I'm so sorry. You should have warned me. He's still suspicious of strangers. Look, he was only frightened." She patted Casanova's head and the horse looked the picture of docility. Sigi tried to reassemble his dignity and spoke sternly.

"Mr. Shooter has just been here, Marianne."

"What did he want?"

"He came to advise us to have the horse destroyed. He says it is incurably vicious."

"What did you say, Dad?" Marny plaited her fingers with worry as she waited for her father's reply. If only Casanova hadn't snapped at him on his first visit. "Stand still, boy," she whispered to the horse. His fate rested on her father's decision.

"I must tell you, Marianne, that I formed a very unfavourable impression of Mr. Shooter."

"You *did,* Daddy?" Marny's expression began to brighten.

"Yes. Actually I have decided that you can keep the horse for the time being. Your mother has told me what really happened. It was extremely brave of you to bring him home. But at the first sign of trouble—he goes. And I don't expect your school marks to fall off either."

"Dad, they won't. They won't. I promise you." Marny was almost dancing with relief and joy. "You do understand why he snapped just now, don't you? He's nervous."

"Marianne, I am not completely ignorant of equine psychology, whatever you may think of me. Now I must go. I have a clinic to attend at ten."

Marny stood hugging Casanova. The first hurdle was safely passed: she could keep him—even though her father had said he was on trial. But she felt sure she could tame him. The next step was to get Mark Thomas to look him over. She refused to look ahead further than that.

Ugly Duckling had been out hunting rabbits when Casanova had arrived. Now he came jauntily into the yard, his tail perpendicular, expecting to find his comfortable box empty and waiting for him. After a successful hunt he needed a good snooze. But when he leapt on to the stable partition, he saw to his indignation that a large strange beast was occupying what the cat considered to be his own private quarters. The striped fur rose on his back until he doubled his size, then he hissed and gave a low warning growl. The horse, startled, half reared and struck out with his forefeet. The cat hissed again and spat. The two animals watched each other closely. Both were seasoned fighters. There was a pause. Then, slowly, the horse stretched out his long neck and smelt the cat. His warm breath ruffled the huffed-up fur, which gradually flattened until Ugly Duckling was back to his normal puny size. Ignoring Casanova, the cat then began to wash himself, one leg cocked behind his ear. The horse pulled placidly at his hay-net, letting straws fall to the ground.

Marny kept her word to her father, and although she spent every spare minute with Casanova, she continued to work hard at school. She never went to Shooter's Riding Academy. Alex was the loser because Marny had done as much as a paid groom and had, besides, been teaching some of the beginners' classes. The pupils missed her. Only Alice was pleased by Marny's absence, which left her unrivalled queen of all the riders.

Towards the end of the term, Mark and Melissa Thomas returned from their trip to Europe. "Let us invite all the Thomases here for Saturday afternoon," Trudy suggested. "I'll do a big baking."

"Great idea, Mum. They haven't seen Casanova, and Mark could examine him at the same time."

When the day came, the Thomas brothers arrived with their wives and children all crowded together in Mark's old station wagon. Trudy felt a stab of envy to see that Candida had proudly brought Barry along with them. "Such a nice young man," she thought. "When will it be Marny's turn?"

Everyone went first to the paddock where Casanova was standing with his head over the gate, watching their arrival with ears pricked.

"Gosh, he looks grand!" said Candida.

"And he's quieter," added Barry, who remembered Casanova from his days at the Shooter stables.

"Have you ridden him yet, Marny?" Janey asked. "Come here at once, children!" The Thomas children were scrambling everywhere.

"They're all right, Mrs. Thomas," said Marny. "They shouldn't run in the paddock, though. Casanova startles easily. No, I haven't ridden him. I exercise him on the lunge and he's in the paddock in the daytime. He's terribly nervous. I don't dare to ride him yet."

"You'll have to soon, won't you? You can't keep a horse you can't ride."

This was a sore point, and Marny was glad when Paul Thomas cried out, "Look at that cat!" Ugly Duckling had jumped on to Casanova's back and was perched in the middle of it, kneading his paws up and down and purring. The horse took no notice of the massage.

"Have you ever seen a sight like that!" exclaimed Janey.

"There have been cat-and-horse friendships before," replied her husband, Andrew. "There's a story about a famous Arab stallion who had a cat for a friend."

"How did that happen?" the children asked.

"Gather round and I'll tell you." Everyone sat in a long line on the paddock rail, with Andrew in the middle, and Casanova stood in front of them as if he was listening too.

"No one knows all the facts of this story because it happened a long time ago. One day the Sultan of Morocco sent six perfect Arab stallions as a present to the King of France, Louis the Fourteenth. When the horses arrived, after a long sea voyage,

60

they were starved and thin. At that time very few people in Europe had seen Arab horses, and they did not appreciate how valuable they were. The courtiers laughed at the thin, small-sized horses. "The great King cannot keep these miserable animals," they said.

"Gradually, the horses were given away or sold. One of them, a high-crested golden bay, could gallop faster than the wind; but nobody in France knew that except his Arab groom—and he was dumb. The stallion had many adventures in France and changed owners several times. Too spirited to be a working horse, he kicked his way out of carts and threw off riders. The little Arab groom followed him wherever he went, sleeping in stables and working for nothing just to stay with his horse."

"But what about the cat?" called out Louise, Candy's youngest sister.

"I'm coming to that. The cat was a Parisian alley-cat that made friends with the horse in his unhappiest days. He used to wait for him to return from work, and he slept with him in his miserable stable. One day a Quaker took pity on the starving carthorse. He bought him and took him to England."

"What did the cat do?"

"The cat went as well. The Arab boy took him wrapped in his cloak, and they lived for a time in the country.

"After more adventures the boy and the cat and the horse found a home with a kind nobleman who bred racehorses. But one day, when a beautiful mare came to the nobleman's stallion, the Arab boy let the golden horse out of his stable. The two stallions fought, and the golden horse won and covered the mare himself. So he and his friends were in disgrace and were sent away to live in a dismal swamp.

"The beautiful mare had a foal by the golden stallion. When the colt was two years old he was watching the nobleman's young racehorses being trained. He jumped out of his field and raced them, beating all other two-year-olds by many lengths. And then at last everyone realised the value of the golden horse, his father. He came back to the stud in triumph and became the chief stallion there. His sons and daughters became famous racehorses."

"What was his name?"

"No one knew his real name, because his pedigree had been lost and the Moroccan lad couldn't tell anyone who he really was. The horse became known as the Godolphin Arabian because his owner was the Earl of Godolphin. There's a beautiful painting of the horse with his friend the cat beside him...."

"But I've heard of the Godolphin Arabian," said Marny excitedly. "He was one of the three horses whose blood runs in the pedigree of all Thoroughbreds."

"That's right," said Mark.

"Do you suppose Casanova is a distant descendant?" she asked. "It's not impossible, is it? He's the right colour."

"*He* hasn't any papers either, and he has a cat for a friend," said Paul.

"Let's hope his story has just as happy an ending," said Louise.

"I shall make sure it does," Marny told them. By now the younger children were clamouring for their tea, so everyone jumped down from the paddock rail and went up to the house. Marny led Casanova into his stable for Mark's check-up.

"He certainly looks a hundred per cent improved since I saw him at Alex Shooter's," said Mark. "His coat has grown, too. But what's this scar on his ear?" Marny wasn't going to say, and wisely Mark did not insist. He knew some of Alex's methods for extracting obedience from a too-spirited horse.

"His teeth need filing," Mark told Marny. He fastened the gag-bit against the horse's teeth and slowly levered the cumbersome gadget open, revealing the badly worn and uneven tables.

"He isn't a day over six," said the vet.

Marny was thrilled by this information. "That's what I thought. He has his whole life ahead of him. D'you think I can do it? Train him, I mean."

"I don't know." Mark rasped down on a projecting molar. "It's going to be hard work for someone, but you've done wonders already."

Casanova stood still throughout the operation while Marny whispered soothingly to him. Mark was satisfied with his work as he withdrew the gag carefully and watched the horse grind his newly-rasped teeth together.

"Remember Sunshine's teeth, Marny?"

"Of course I do."

"If this horse turns out so well we'll be lucky."

Next was a drench. Marny was preoccupied in watching Mark mix the drench in a quart-can and oil the small rubber drenching tube, ready to insert it into the horse's nostrils. Ugly Duckling chose this moment to jump down from the stable partition and knock an empty tin off the wall with a clatter.

"Get that damned cat out of here," Mark shouted. At the sound of the shout Casanova was alerted. He did not attack as he would have done some weeks ago, but his ears flattened and he showed the whites of his eyes. Marny spoke gently to the horse. She knew what he could do if he was frightened and aroused. If he attacked Mark now, her father would never let him stay. Mark stood back. The contest of wills was between the slight girl and her horse: it was Marny's affair.

Casanova jerked his halter out of Marny's hand and backed to the corner of the box. "Steady boy, steady," she said calmly. "We're all your friends. Come on." Without stopping the flow of soothing words, she went right up to him. At first Casanova stood rigid with suspicion. Then, as he sniffed her outstretched palm, he blew softly through his nostrils. He allowed Marny to pat him and lead him back to the front of the box, then he lowered his head, nudging her hand as if he were a family pony asking for sugar. The laid-back ears straightened out and pricked up with interest.

"Good girl," Mark said shortly.

After the interruption, Casanova behaved perfectly, allowing the drench tube to be passed up his nostril and down into his gullet. Mark waited until the tube had been swallowed, and listened for the sound of the liquid gurgling in the horse's stomach.

"Always take care that you by-pass the lungs when you're drenching," he told Marny. Next, he took a blood sample to test whether the horse was anaemic. After he had listened to the heartbeat, he passed the stethoscope to Marny so that she could listen.

"He has a ticker like a long-distance runner. He's sound as a bell. Only a bit thin, and that's easily altered. I can't find anything wrong with him organically. He must have been sent to the slaughter yard simply because of his bad temper."

Marny was delighted with Mark's diagnosis. They linked arms and went up to the house for their tea.

"What a crazy cat that turned out to be," said Mark.

"I know," she replied, grinning.

The sitting-room was full of laughter and the clink of teacups. Trudy, Marny, and Candida ran to and fro between the kitchen and the sitting-room, refilling plates. Melissa was telling Janey about her visit to Greece. "It was wonderful seeing my aunts and uncles. I did not recognise some of the children. But I'm not sorry Mark has made Armidale home for me now."

Mark smiled at her, then turned to Sigi." That horse of Marny's ought to have a great future. He's sound and he's got good blood."

"Yes, yes," said Sigi fussily. "I know he looks splendid, but how is Marny going to train him? She hasn't enough experience. And if we don't find a solution he'll have to go."

Marny looked anxious when she heard her father talk like that. She thought Casanova's trial period was already over.

"Don't look so worried," Candida whispered soothingly. "Your dad's bark is worse than his bite. I'm sure he doesn't really mean it."

Micky, the baby, was sitting almost in the empty fireplace with a jam tart in one hand and a sticky bottle of orange cordial in the other. Marny watched him affectionately, then jumped up in horror as she saw him deposit his half-eaten tart in the middle of a book lying open on the carpet beside him.

"Do be careful, Micky," she cried. "That's Alice's book, and if you make it dirty she'll be furious."

She carefully rubbed traces of jam off the page with a rather grubby handkerchief, and as she did so her eyes were caught by the caption to a photograph: "Note the faultless position and style of Tibor Szechy, European jumping champion 1932 and 1937, riding Capriole." Candida peered over her shoulder. "What a beautiful horse," she said longingly. "Look, Mark."

She passed the book over to her uncle, and he studied the photograph carefully, his face creased with concentration. "That's funny. Marny, does this man's face look familiar to you?"

"No. What a lovely style, though. I wish I could ride like that."

Mark looked thoughtful. "Do you remember coming with me to Glen Innes last winter? That old man with the pig farm. His name was Szechy."

"It couldn't be the same person, could it?" said Marny, beginning to feel excited.

"I went there again," said Mark. "He had two photos in the kitchen. One was of a white horse doing some sort of funny trot. I asked him how long it took to train a horse to do that, and all he said was, 'A lifetime, Mr. Thomas.'"

"Are there white horses on the farm now?" asked Susy.

"There isn't a horse on the place. He lives completely alone."

"But, Mark," interrupted Candida, "surely if there was a famous champion rider living in our district we would have heard of him?"

"No," said Sigi. "I understand. Australia is a big country. People come here for many reasons. Some want to forget their past lives. Perhaps Tibor Szechy is one of them."

"Have you heard of him, Dad?"

"No, I haven't."

Trudy spoke up. "I have, *Liebchen*. Before the war, in Vienna. There *was* a famous show-jumper. He used to be with the Spanish Riding School, and he left finally to breed and show his own horses. My brother knew him."

Marny pored over the photograph, trying to see in this graceful young rider the face of the courteous old man she dimly recalled from the year before. An idea too thrilling to be spoken aloud had begun to form in her mind.

"How can we find out if it *is* the same man?"

"We can't, unless we go and ask him," said Mark. "He is reserved. I don't think he likes strangers."

Trudy guessed what was in her daughter's mind. She said practically, "Glen Innes is over a hundred kilometres away. How could you get the horse there?"

"We must find a way," said Marny, her green eyes glowing.

Chapter 10

Saturday 7 July. Marny had marked the date in her diary—the day on which she was to meet Tibor Szechy, one-time European jumping champion and now an unknown pig farmer in Glen Innes. She fussed around the stable waiting for Mark while Casanova ate his usual breakfast: 1·5 kilos of oats and nearly half a kilo of bran. His ribby look was vanishing and the hollows on his back were filling out.

When Mark arrived, he looked with approval at the clean stable and the silky horse. "You're a good stable manager, Marny. Do you know the saying, 'The eye of the master maketh the horse fat'?" Marny didn't, and could hardly concentrate on what Mark was saying.

"I'm afraid we've got some work to do first. Fifty cows for T.B. testing. Relax! We won't take too long, and Szechy won't run away."

"Will he like Casanova, do you think?"

"He has to like *you* first. If he's the man I think he is, he'll understand the horse."

They got into the old station wagon and set off. Today Marny didn't even notice the paddocks flashing past. She sat silent and preoccupied. Would Tibor Szechy like her? Would a champion want to train a schoolgirl? Why hadn't he worked with horses in Australia before? What would she say to him? She wriggled uncomfortably in her seat, her thoughts increasingly gloomy. Mark, glancing at her taut little face, tugged at a lock of her hair.

"Snap out of it, lass. Che *sarà sarà.*"

"What does that mean?"

"What will be, will be."

The cattle to be tested for T.B. were on a farm eight kilometres beyond Glen Innes. The previous night's rain had turned the yard into quagmire and the cattle crush was fifteen centimetres deep in red mud. Each cow was pushed along the crush, bled, sampled, recorded, and released into the adjoining paddock. Marny and Mark worked fast and finished in under two hours. Marny was covered in mud, her hair blown into a tangle.

"Hadn't you better clean up too?" she asked Mark anxiously, when the farmer's wife took her inside for a wash.

"I'm all right," he laughed. "I'm not going to a fashion show."

The farmer thanked them warmly before they left. "That lassie is a good worker," he told Mark. "She can have a job here any time she wants one."

They drove back through the small town of Glen Innes, turning east along a three-kilometre dirt road to Szechy's farm. The rainfall was higher here than in Armidale and the gum trees grew taller. Tibor's property covered only eight hectares, but it was well kept and prosperous. Leafless Banksia rose and wistaria clung to the walls of the little cottage. Marny imagined that in spring they would make it pretty with their yellow and mauve flowers, but at this season everything looked sparse and bleak. She felt butterflies swooping in her stomach. A slimly-built old man was approaching them, limping badly. She leaned against the car door, pressing her hands together firmly to stop them trembling.

"This," said Mark, "is Marianne Mann. The girl I told you about."

"Welcome, Miss Mann." She looked into the old man's wrinkled face, not recognising it from the photograph in Alice's book. This face was thinner, and the deepset eyes above the broad, Slavic cheekbones were dark brown and compelling. Tibor Szechy had a strong Hungarian accent. He shook Marny's damp palm firmly.

"You're taller since last year." Marny nodded, not knowing what to say.

68

Tibor seemed to understand. "Come into the house," he said, leading the way. "We shall drink coffee and discuss your problem. I live alone, you see." Marny glanced curiously around the simple room, undecorated except for a row of silver-framed photographs on the mantelpiece. "Forgive my English, young lady. It's not so fine."

"But you speak awfully fine, I mean well," said Marny, adding shyly, "My parents came from Europe, too. But I was born in Armidale."

"Ah, so. That explains your Australian name." He made them both sit down, motioning Mark into the only comfortable armchair, before seating himself on an upright wooden one. "You have some problems with your pony?"

"Not quite a pony. Actually, he's a bit over sixteen two."

"Ah, so," Tibor said again, looking pleased. "What is the trouble with the animal?"

Marny briefly told the old man the story of how she had lost Sure Smile and acquired Casanova. "And now," she concluded, "I'm stuck. He's quiet enough in the stable, but I don't have enough experience to train him." She was gradually forgetting her shyness. "My dad won't let me keep him unless he's schooled, and I can't do that alone. We were desperate until we found out about who you really are. You're our only hope."

"Is the horse a Thoroughbred?"

"Through and through," Mark replied. "We've no papers, but you'll only have to look at him. It's all there—the lines and the courage."

"Good." Tibor turned to Marny. "What do you want the horse to become?"

"A show jumper," came the prompt reply.

The old man looked grave. "I can promise nothing. I have not trained horses for many years." He paused, then continued slowly, "Bring Casanova here next Saturday. I shall give an answer after I have seen him."

"Oh, *thank* you!" Marny said. "I know you won't regret it."

Driving home through the chilly winter dusk, the headlights of the station wagon fleetingly illuminating scuttling rabbits,

Mark said, "I've never seen him work a horse. He's a first-rate pig farmer though. I'd trust him with anything."

"I would, too. He looks so sad, though."

"Probably with reason."

When they arrived back at the Mann household and told Marny's parents that Tibor had asked to see the horse, Sigi was delighted. "I'll be glad to have an expert's opinion," he said.

"Such a wild horse." Trudy shook her head. "So wild."

Marny hadn't yet told her parents that she had no idea how she was going to take Casanova all the way up to Glen Innes. On Monday, as they were travelling to school on the bus, she and Candida considered the problem.

"Mr. Shooter hires out his small trailer," suggested Candida.

Marny shook her head. "After what he tried to do to Cas, I never want anything to do with him again," she said seriously.

"That's understandable," replied her friend. "Look, let me try an idea."

"What is it?"

Candida grinned. "Don't nag. I won't tell you yet. Promise I will soon."

"There are so many obstacles ahead," Marny sighed.

"Isn't that what you want? I thought Cas was going to be a show jumper."

Then, abruptly, she changed the subject. "You'll have to do *something* about Blair," she said. "He's been hanging around at the bus stop for weeks waiting to see you, and you hardly notice him."

"I know," Marny agreed, miserably. "He's very nice, but when I've been busy with Cas—I don't seem interested in him."

"You're sixteen, Marny. When *are* you going to grow up?"

"I dunno. What do you think I should do?"

"Go out with him again. Try to be more friendly."

Marny agreed in a rather half-hearted way, and Candida ran back to the classroom, smiling mischievously. Her plots were hatching out.

When Blair sauntered up to the school bus stop at three-thirty that afternoon, pretending he was just passing, he received a warm smile.

"Gosh, Marny, you look happy."

She told him the good news about Tibor Szechy.

"That's great!" Blair was glad that at last someone would help Marny with her savage horse. "Will you come out with me on Saturday night to celebrate?"

Marny looked rather confused, not knowing what to reply, and Candida seized the opportunity to butt in, saying, "Why don't we go out in a foursome? Barry and I are going to the pictures."

"Great," replied Blair. But Marny whispered to her friend, "Promise you'll really come."

"Of course I will!"

"O.K.," said Marny decisively. "I would love to come out with you, Blair."

"Beaut! See you then. Pick you up at your place at seven," and he headed off for the playing fields. He wasn't going to be late for football practice *again,* now that Marny had finally agreed to go out with him.

"I hope I've done the right thing, Candy. I haven't gone out with anyone since Sure Smile's accident."

"About time too," was the cheerful reply. "You can't go to the pictures with a horse, can you?"

"Don't be silly," Marny laughed. She ought to have felt more excited at the prospect of going out with a boy as popular as Blair, but she wasn't. At home she forgot about him because one of Casanova's hind shoes was loose and she had to take him to the blacksmith.

Next day, Candida still refused to tell Marny her plan for borrowing a float. "Don't worry," she said. "Something will turn up."

Marny decided, in the face of her friend's obstinacy, that she would have to telephone Mark Thomas for advice. But Candida proved right. Something *did* turn up, and she never had to make her telephone call after all.

That evening, when she got off the school bus to walk home, she found a blue utility parked at her stop. The window was rolled down and a fair head poked through.

"Hullo, Marny. Can I give you a lift?"

She stared incredulously. "What are *you* doing here?" She had not seen Peter Cooke-Finch since the day they had taken Casanova around to Alex Shooter's.

"Oh, I was just passing. Hop in. There's something I want to talk to you about."

"*Talk* to me about?"

"That's what I said. Do hop in." Marny obeyed. Her heart seemed to be thumping peculiarly.

"It's about borrowing a float," Peter said as they drove off. "Mrs. Rowbotham's got one and she's willing to lend it."

"Mrs. Rowbotham? A float? You're joking!"

"I'm not, Scout's honour. She bought it a couple of years ago when she started riding at Shooter's. But she's never used it, so it's been standing idle in her shed. It's quite sound, just a bit dusty. We've seen it."

"We've seen it? Who's 'we'?"

"Me and Candy."

"You and *Candy?*"

"Look, stop repeating everything I say."

"I'm *not* repeating everything you say." She began to feel annoyed. "Why are you and Candy meddling in my affairs?"

"Marny." Peter spoke softly.

"What!"

"Don't you know why?"

"No, I don't!"

"Don't you know that I've liked you since the first time we met....at Blair's party?"

"But you spent the evening with Alice!"

"Oh, Marny. Why *are* you so naive? Isn't anyone else except you ever supposed to be shy?"

Marny glanced at the tall boy sitting beside her. Then she said slowly, "I'm sorry if I sounded ungrateful. Please forgive me. It's just....just that I...."

"Well, let's not talk about that any more. Let's just be friends. Mrs. Rowbotham to the rescue!"

"But what about the towing?"

"Problem solved already. We had a towbar fixed to this car last night."

"You mean you and Candy settled everything behind my back?"

"That's right. Are you cross?"

The car drew up outside the Mann house, and Marny thought, "This whole scene has only lasted two minutes." Then she jumped out of the car before Peter could stop her.

"No! I'm not!" she called back to him. "I'm rather glad!"

Chapter 11

Marny wisped Casanova with plaited straw until every particle of dust left his coat. With his rug on and his legs protected by stable bandages, he had been prepared like a film star going off for an important audition. All his friends assembled in the stable yard to watch his departure. Mrs. Rowbotham arrived first and squashed herself on to a shooting stick directly in front of the horse's box, and Blair, the next arrival, pulled a hay bale out of the shed and sat down beside her. It was kind of them to wish her well, but Marny felt irritable and tense as they both watched her every movement with goggle eyes. Candida rode into the yard on Moonlight with Louise riding pillion, but when she saw Marny's strained expression she wisely kept quiet. Mark Thomas and Janey drove up with Melissa on their way into town. Everyone admired Casanova.

"You don't have to wait," Marny told Blair, knowing that he had football practice that morning.

"Righty-ho," said Blair happily. "Best of luck," and he cycled away, whistling out of tune.

It hadn't occurred to Marny that Blair didn't know Peter Cooke-Finch was driving her to Glen Innes. The blue utility swung into the drive ten minutes after Blair had left. "Don't worry," Peter called to Trudy. "We're not late!"

"Careful of the dear gee-gee going into the box," warned Mrs. Rowbotham. Casanova must have heard her. Marny led him confidently up to the ramp; he could see his hay-net hanging enticingly in the interior. Then, suddenly, he stopped dead and started to back. Half a ton of solid horseflesh—immobile. Marny pulled, pushed, coaxed, and pleaded, but with everyone crowding round offering advice, and Whisky barking, Casanova was convinced that his misgivings were wellfounded—the float *was* a suspicious object, and one a sensible horse should avoid. He laid his ears back.

"Now what do we do?"

"Haul him up with a rope round his quarters."

"Use a stick." "Try a carrot." "Take it slowly." "Hurry him up."

Candida rode into the circle of excited people. "Let me try," she demanded. Dismounting, she lifted Louise down and, pulling Moonlight behind her, ran lightly up the ramp and into the box. The cob followed her placidly and began munching hay without even waiting for his bridle to be taken off. He loved travelling in floats.

"Come on boy," Marny pleaded to Casanova. "See how easy it is!" Casanova considered the situation for a moment, then, lowering his head, walked calmly up the ramp into the float and took his place beside Moonlight, taking alternate pulls at the hay-net.

The spectators clapped and cheered, and the noise brought Ugly Duckling into the yard to investigate. Ignoring everybody, he stalked past them and leapt straight into the float. A second leap carried him on to the chestnut's back; the serge rug rumpled up and then smoothed down as the cat balanced himself.

Peter turned to Candida. "Seems we've two extra passengers aboard. Can Moonlight come with us? He'll keep Cas calm."

"Sure," answered Candida with relief. "Louise and I can drive home with Uncle Mark."

"Gracious me!" exclaimed Mrs. Rowbotham, snapping shut her shooting stick. "What a performance! Did you practise it?"

Finally Peter raised the ramp, enclosed the tail-gate, and they were off, to the accompaniment of more hearty cheers and good wishes.

The early morning frost had thawed and it was a brilliantly sunny winter's day. Tibor Szechy, having heard the float approaching down the dirt road, was already waiting for them, holding open the gate so they could drive through. He greeted them politely, seeming not to notice their casual clothes. Although Marny had spent hours preparing her horse, she hadn't thought of herself; and she wore her usual jeans and skivvy. Tibor looked like an illustration in an old-fashioned riding manual, formally dressed in breeches and boots with a jacket and tie and a soft cap.

"Isn't it silly dressing up just for training?" Marny whispered to Peter, her face red. Peter didn't reply. He was thinking that if Marny wanted Tibor to be her trainer, she would have to accept his traditions: correct riding dress appeared to be one of them. He made a private resolution to look less scruffy himself next time.

After they had finished exchanging greetings, Peter let down the ramp and Marny led out the horses in turn.

"There appears to be a cat left inside," said Tibor.

"Oh, that's Ugly Duckling," said Marny. "He won't leave Casanova alone." Ugly Duckling sprang out and made his way purposefully towards the barn. He smelt rats there.

Tibor walked slowly round Casanova as Marny took off his rugs. She tried to see her horse through the expert's eyes, noting with appreciation the elegant head with its large well-shaped eyes and small sharp ears pricked forward. Casanova's neck was beginning to build up and his mane flowed gently across his developing crest. He had sloping shoulders and well-defined withers with a deep, broad chest and ribs well sprung out of a short back. His quarters would be massive when he reached peak condition. His legs were fine and clean with plenty of bone and hocks well let down. But more than just good conformation, Casanova had presence.

"Do you like him?" Marny asked nervously.

Tibor frowned at the interruption and continued to walk round the horse. Peter squeezed her arm and whispered, "Don't worry. He likes him."

"We will start," said Tibor, apparently satisfied. "Have you the lunge equipment?"

Marny started rummaging furiously in the back of the utility. Why hadn't she put everything tidily together? She handed the

77

gear to Tibor while Peter led Moonlight away to graze. Tibor fixed the cavesson over Casanova's head, but left off the side-reins. Then he began to lead him into a small field behind the pig sheds.

Casanova smelled the pigs—an unfamiliar smell. He rolled his eyes at the stranger quietly leading him past the sheds and decided not to accept the situation. Rearing up, he flailed his hooves in the air, dropped suddenly, bucked, and reared again. The man held steadily on to the lunge-line. Casanova completed the second rear, then bunched himself together and leapt up with all four legs in the air, kicking out savagely with his hind feet. Although he made a beautiful sight, Marny was horrified. As Casanova lowered his head, ready for some more bucking, he expected to hear the panic-filled shouts that usually greeted his displays. But Tibor only smiled and tut-tutted. Had the man gone mad? No! He was merely enjoying the spirit and grace of the Thoroughbred, not at all concerned—until the moment arrived to show who was master. When Casanova reared for the third time he received a forceful jerk on the cavesson. He stopped abruptly, his nose stinging, and looked around suspiciously. The man waited calmly. Maybe there was no real danger — only a peculiar *smell*....He didn't want to hurt himself. Was there any need to fight? He rubbed his nose against the stranger's arm and licked salt stains off his leather glove while Tibor continued his soothing murmur in a language neither Casanova nor Marny knew.

"Walk on," he commanded firmly, and the chestnut obeyed. Tibor played out the lunge-line until the horse was striding freely on a twenty-metre circle, his haunches swinging, controlled between the whip and the lunge-rein. The trainer insisted that the walk never deviate from its four-beat rhythm. Watching the first few minutes of the lesson, Marny realised one of her errors when she lunged Cas at home: he walked faster towards the stable than away from it. But Tibor kept the horse at a steady, even pace throughout the exercise.

At the command "Trot on," Casanova swung into his ground-covering trot. Tibor's face was expressionless.

Marny's palms were sticky with sweat. "How do you think it's going?" she asked Peter.

"I'm not sure yet. Keep quiet and watch them."

"Can....ter....!" Casanova launched into an unsteady canter on the left lead. After his free trot, his pace was now awkward and unbalanced. Tibor watched closely for a few circles, then brought him to a halt. He patted him and sent him off in a canter on the right lead. This time the movement was better, more balanced and graceful. Tibor smiled to see his suspicions confirmed. Casanova must have been trained as a racehorse and so had always galloped to the right, in an anti-clockwise direction. The horse gave a little buck and Tibor let him play. From this first encounter a special teacher-pupil relationship was being established.

"You have done quite well," was Tibor's verdict when the lesson finished.

"Whew!" Marny sighed with relief. "I'm so glad you think so. Does it mean that you will help us?"

The old man said grimly, "I'm not sure. That must be discussed."

Peter and Marny looked at one another with dismay. Peter shrugged his shoulders. No one spoke, and Marny's eyes were smarting as they led Cas back to the house and put him to graze with Moonlight.

"Don't worry," said Peter comfortingly. "It'll be allright. He just wants time to think things over."

Tibor seemed almost angry, although Marny couldn't imagine what they had done wrong. But when they reached the house he said, "Would you care to lunch with me?"

"But we've got our sandwiches in the car," Marny exclaimed.

"It would be an honour for me to entertain you," Tibor replied formally. He led them indoors, and they discovered that the table in the farm kitchen had been laid for four.

"You *meant* us to stay!" Marny cried, delighted. Surely this was a good sign.

"Not *meant,* young lady. But *hoped,*" said Tibor Szechy. As he smiled, his stern expression vanished.

"Who is the fourth place for, sir?" asked Peter.

"Me," said a familiar voice as Mark Thomas came through the doorway, smiling broadly. "How did it go? What's the training programme to be?"

Marny said sadly, "We don't know. Mr. Szechy hasn't agreed to take us on. We're just hoping."

"First, let us sit down and eat," said the host. "And Miss Mann....stop looking so tragic. I am going to train you and your horse."

Marny smiled and smiled. She couldn't say a thing. Peter winked at her and Tibor said, "I hope you like this. It is a goulash—the only dish I know how to cook." The meal was delicious.

They were drinking a light South Australian wine and Marny, who had begged a glassful, began to feel slightly woozy. A delightful future stretched before her....jumping, ribbons, cups, success....A dry voice interrupted her daydreams. "It will not be like that, Miss Mann. The work with that horse will be hard—hard and monotonous. He has to learn much. Above all, to trust us. It cannot be easy. Have you enough patience and stamina?"

"Yes, of course. I zink zo. So zorry. I mean I think so." She wasn't trying to copy Tibor's Hungarian accent; it was the wine. She explained rapidly, "There's no one in Armidale who knows about training like you do. I've read books. That's how we knew you were you. But it's not the same thing, is it?"

Tibor seemed to understand her confused remarks. Mark said, "She's right you know, Szechy. If you take her on, it'll be great for all of us."

"I thank you for your confidence in me," said Tibor, bowing slightly. "When I first heard your request I wanted to refuse. The years have been too long. You were not born, Marny, when I stopped riding."

Marny stood up shakily. "Mr. Szechy, you must have had good reasons *then,* but please—come back to horses *now.* We need you. There is so much you can teach us."

"I have accepted, Marianne."

Mark, embarrassed by all the emotion floating over his lunch, interrupted heartily: "Who's for more wine?"

"I've had 'nuff already," said Marny, and she began to cry on Peter's shoulder. Tibor was hardly disconcerted: a pretty girl weeping only reminded him of his days as a dashing young cavalry officer in Hungary. He said cheerfully, "I suggest you take Miss Mann home, Peter. Bring her tomorrow for another lesson. Same time?"

"Certainly, sir. What shall I do about the horses?"

"They will stay here overnight. The garage converts easily into a stable."

Peter guessed that Tibor Szechy must have decided to accept Marny from the beginning, and had simply been testing her out to discover how keen she really was. "Mark must have been pretty persuasive," he thought. "Still, anyone would want to help Marny."

That young lady was still sniffing back the sobs as they drove off, leaving Mark and Tibor, satisfied with their morning's work, to finish off the bottle of wine.

Chapter 12

Marny and Peter drove back to Armidale in friendly silence, both too full of the day's events to want to talk. The return journey without the float behind them was far quicker than the trip out.

"We're home," said Marny, stating the obvious. "Are you coming in for tea?"

"Sorry, I can't. Got an assignment I must finish."

"What's it on?"

"A farm budget. Bit of a bore, actually. I'm sorry for the farmers who have to do them in real life."

"You will soon, I suppose, when you graduate?"

"And you'll be doing farm budgets at university."

"No, I'll be doing rabbits' bloodstreams. It seems an awfully long time away."

"Only fourteen months," Peter reminded her. He leant across to open the car door. "It's not so long really." They smiled at each other.

"See you tomorrow morning early!" Peter called out as she ran indoors.

Trudy bustled up, full of questions and curiosity. "Blair phoned," she said. "He'll be here at seven-thirty, so you've only an hour to get ready."

"Oh, Mum!" Marny clapped her hand to her mouth. "I can't *possibly* go—not after Peter."

Trudy took no notice. "Darling, go and change. You'll be late."

"Leave me alone, Mum," Marny snapped. She rushed off to her room, leaving her mother staring. "Oh well," she said to Sigi, "I suppose girls are moody at that age."

Blair arrived punctually, but no Marny was in sight, so Trudy asked him to wait for a few minutes in Sigi's study. The minutes stretched to five, ten, fifteen....still no Marny. Blair and Trudy and Sigi had used up all their small talk and were staring miserably at one another, until Trudy excused herself and ran down the hall to her daughter's bedroom. She found Marny face downwards on the bed, her head buried under the pillow.

"Blair's been here for twenty minutes. You *can't* keep him waiting any longer."

Marny mumbled "no" sounds from beneath the pillow.

"Marny, you *must*. What's the matter? Why won't you?"

"Please don't make me, Mum. Say I'm ill. I never bothered with boyfriends, and now I've got two. I can't cope."

Trudy laughed understandingly. "Is *that* all that's worrying you?" She sat beside Marny and stroked her hair. "*Liebchen,* don't get upset. It's not so unusual to have one boy like you when you like someone else. But that is not a reason to break your promises and be rude to him. Now go out and enjoy yourself. You can explain to Blair. He's a nice boy. He will understand."

Marny sat up and managed a shaky smile. "Mum, you're right. I'm being silly." She got up and started to change. Since Sure Smile's accident Marny had altered. Her gawkiness was turning into slenderness, and the blue striped dress she now wore made her look more grown-up than she really was.

"You *are* worth waiting for," Blair commented, standing up to greet her.

Marny blushed. "Don't be silly. Come on, let's go." She kissed her parents. "Don't wait up for me, Mum. 'Night."

"Ah, Sigi," said Trudy sentimentally when the front door had closed. "Doesn't it take you back a bit?"

Sigi looked at his plump, grey-haired little wife. "Yes, *Liebchen.* But you're still as pretty as you were in those days."

Candida and Barry were waiting outside the Thomas' gate when Blair roared up in his borrowed Moke. The engine coughed and stalled.

84

"Sorry, Marny. I haven't got the hang of it yet." Blair's licence was only two months old, and this was the first time he had driven at night. The other two squashed into the back, and after two false starts, Blair got the Moke going again.

"Wouldn't a horse be easier?" asked Marny.

"Maybe. But I won't bet on Moke versus Cas," said Blair. "After all, Cas is always rearing, isn't he?"

"Sometimes. But he doesn't stop dead every hundred metres."

The Moke had stalled again. This time it was out of petrol. The boys got out and pushed it to a garage while Candida steered. They reached the cinema just after the film had started, and the two boys bought seats in the back row. Marny hoped Blair wouldn't want to kiss her. But fortunately it was a war film and Blair became so engrossed that he forgot about romance.

"It's too early for home. Where shall we go?" asked Barry, once the film was over.

"How about the Athens?" suggested Candida.

"Good idea! Let's walk—it's only three blocks," Blair replied.

"He's worried about starting the car," thought Marny, suddenly realising how nervous Blair was. She felt sorry for him— he was trying so hard. Tapping him on the arm, she said, "Come on—race you there."

They burst into the Athens café dishevelled and laughing. Nicolas Theopoulos, the proprietor, was an old friend of Melissa's: twenty years earlier, they had come to Australia together. When Nick started his café all Melissa's friends and relatives became patrons. It was an unpretentious place, with Formica tables and a blow-up of Athens along one wall, but Nick served the best food in the district. He catered for his Greek customers by playing *bouzouki* music on the jukebox.

"What will you have, my friends?" he asked, raising his eyebrows to see Marny out so late at night. Marny leant back in her chair with a sophisticated air and thought about taking one of Barry's cigarettes. Nick winked at her and made her giggle.

"O.K., Nick. I give up. Same as usual for me."

They all had coffee and Greek pastries dripping with honey and smothered in nuts. It was hopeless anyway trying to put on

85

a sophisticated manner between mouthfuls of gooey honey. Everyone wanted a second helping.

The others asked eagerly about the trip to Glen Innes. Marny tried to tell them, but was too covered in honey.

"Wipe your mouth and start again," said Candida.

"What does Mr. Szechy *do* with Cas?"

"You can't explain unless you see them working together. He has him going as sweetly as a child's pony."

"What does the old man look like?" Candida wanted to know.

"Much older than the photograph we saw. He's got beautiful hands, square and very strong, but he's terribly lame."

"Poor chap," mused Barry. "I suppose he can't ride himself."

"I don't know yet. I don't see how he can, because his knee is stiff."

"Did Mark drive the float up?" asked Blair.

There was a silence. Candida looked at Marny.

"Actually, Peter Cooke-Finch drove me in his car. Mark joined us for lunch," Marny explained quietly.

"I see." Blair's face slowly reddened. Although he knew it was ridiculous, he couldn't help feeling jealous. "I thought you said he was a snob. You seem to have had a change of heart."

"I'm sorry I said he was a snob. I was wrong. He's not really stuck-up—he's shy."

Blair was silent, and his silence made Marny feel uncomfortable. She sensed that she had upset him, but didn't know what to say to make things better. Barry and Candida talked loudly and cheerfully, trying to recapture the pleasant mood of the evening, but it was too late. Both Marny and Blair seemed tired and dispirited, and there seemed to be nothing left to do but pay their bill and leave. Then, once again, the car wouldn't start. The battery was flat. Although they pushed it for several metres, nothing happened. "Maybe it's the ignition," Blair said, crossly. By the time they had reached the turn-off where the couples split up to go their separate ways, they were frozen with cold.

Blair walked Marny home. They said goodnight with forced casualness, and Marny went inside and finally crawled into bed, exhausted and depressed. "I do wish I hadn't gone," she told the sympathetic Whisky. "At least there's tomorrow at Glen

Innes–that's something to look forward to. But Blair *is* silly. There was no reason for him to behave like that just because I told him about Peter. I'll never understand boys." But she was too tired to worry about Blair for long, and soon fell asleep with Whisky curled up round her back, keeping them both warm.

The alarm bell rang all too soon, signalling Sunday morning—or rather, later Sunday morning, for Marny had not got to bed until one. Trudy had not slept either, for she had lain awake for hours wondering how her little girl was enjoying her first date. When Peter arrived at eight o'clock, humming cheerfully, he found mother and daughter padding listlessly around the kitchen, absent-mindedly picking things up and putting them down.

"Late night?" he asked callously. "I'd better make you two some coffee." The hot drink scalded Marny's tongue, but she began to feel more wide-awake.

Half an hour later, Trudy hurried them out of the kitchen. "Don't be late," she smiled at Peter. "The master's waiting."

"We won't," Peter called back to her. "The journey's faster without the float. It didn't take two hours yesterday, and it's not half-past eight yet."

"Don't I know it!" replied Trudy, rubbing her still aching head.

"She's nice, your mother," said Peter a little wistfully as they drove away.

"Yes, she is," said Marny sympathetically, knowing that Peter's mother had died the year before he came to Armidale. "I'm lucky," she went on. "My dad's nice too. He's a bit harder to get to know, but he likes you."

"So long as *everyone* does in the Mann household, I'm lucky too."

They arrived early at the farm, but Tibor was already waiting at the gate. He nodded approvingly when he saw Marny's breeches and long rubber riding-boots.

"I'm sorry I don't have proper leather riding-boots, Mr. Szechy," she said. "Will these do?"

"They will be adequate," he replied. "Don't think that correct clothes for riding are an affectation. They are not. Every garment has its purpose, just as every movement we teach the horse has." Marny looked doubtful. "You will see, Miss Mann."

"But why can't I wear...." She started to argue and then stopped, realising how foolish she would sound, arguing with a master. But there was no time for selfconsciousness. Tibor quickly had them organised, bringing out the horses and tacking up Casanova.

Marny saw how beautifully groomed the chestnut had been. His hooves had been oiled and his mane glistened. Tibor did not mention the extra work he must have put in—even Moonlight was gleaming.

They walked Casanova out past the pigs, and this time he did not repeat yesterday's performance. Then Tibor lunged him, at the same time explaining why each action was performed.

"You will need to keep a training log," he told Marny. "You must perform during the week the same exercises I am showing you now, and each weekend you will come here so that I can check on your progress. I hope the young man will lunge the horse when you are doing your mounted exercises."

"Mounted exercises?"

"Of course. What else? This is a riding horse we are training. Or is he meant for driving?"

Tibor's sarcasm made Marny flare up. "Of course not! When do I get to ride him?"

"Now, of course," said Tibor, hiding a smile. Marny's flash of spirit pleased him as much as the horse's fiery temperament. He would enjoy taming and teaching them both.

Asking Peter to hold Casanova, he went back to the house, returning with a well-oiled saddle over his arm.

"You may use my old German saddle," he said. "The seat is hard but it will help you to sit deeply. I have noticed that many Australian saddles are badly built: the deepest part of the cantle is set too far back."

The saddle fitted Cas perfectly.

"Must have been a big horse this saddle was made for." said Peter.

"She was," came the curt reply. They would have liked to know more, but Tibor's expression forbade further questions. Marny legged-up on to Casanova. She felt great.

"There are no stirrups," she said.

"Do you think you need them?"

"Please."

"I don't. Walk on. Correct position please."

Marny was sitting as stiff as a broom handle, tense in every muscle. She held her hands low down on Casanova's neck, her fingers shut tight.

"Relax, Miss Mann. A good rider is never tense." Marny tried to obey, but couldn't. Casanova sensed her discomfort and started to jog. Tibor brought him to a halt and addressed his rider.

"Place your right leg over the pommel of the saddle," he said. Marny stared at him in surprise but did as she was told.

"Now put your right hand on the cantle and your left hand on the pommel," he continued. Marny started to feel most uncomfortable.

"Turn around and rest your tummy against the saddle. Take your right leg over the back of the saddle so that you will be astride again." He had hardly finished the instructions when Marny grunted, trying desperately to get her right leg over the cantle. It was useless. She had slipped too far down and couldn't muster the strength to return to the saddle. She let go, slid inelegantly to the ground, and rolled over. Peter started laughing, and Casanova turned his head to look at her. Tibor was not laughing. His expression was severe, and only a glimmer of amusement showed in his eyes.

"Up again," was his only comment.

"He didn't even ask me if I was all right," Marny thought crossly, her shoulder bruised, her pride wounded. Absolutely determined now, she gritted her teeth and tried again. Deftly she swung out of the saddle and levered her right leg across. "There, that's showed them!" she thought.

"Now again," came the command. Tibor kept her performing the exercise until she had completed it five times to each side, first the right leg over, then the left leg. The faint spark of defiance in Marny had flickered out long ago. She was tired, panting, and grateful to be allowed to rest.

"Good. Now you have a more relaxed seat in the saddle."

"I'm exhausted."

"I hope not. Casanova certainly isn't. Walk on!"

The chestnut strode forward energetically. Marny felt his back swinging beneath her from the first stride.

She tried to sit deeper in the saddle, stretching her legs down to bring her heels a fraction lower. Tibor observed her efforts with pleasure.

"Trot on!" he commanded. He flicked his whip at the horse's left shoulder, which tended to lean inward on the circle. Casanova was annoyed. He stopped dead, lowered his head, and gave a powerful kick with his off hindleg.

"None of that!" the man cautioned firmly, immediately flicking the whip at the kicking leg. Casanova reacted with fury. Was he going back to the old days of fights and blows? He half-reared and flailed his forelegs in the air, prancing on his haunches. Marny had lost her balance at the first kick and was flung forward on to the horse's neck. She clung on tightly. "Steady! steady!" she whispered. But Casanova ignored her. His attention and his defiance were directed at the calm figure in the centre of the circle.

"Trot on!" Tibor repeated firmly as the horse's hooves thudded to the ground. Casanova was faced with an alternative: to advance or to rear. "Trot on!" urged the master. The horse decided to go forward, and plunged into a gallop, oblivious of the light weight on his back. Tibor was placed perfectly to rebuff the headstrong challenge. Casanova caught a nasty jerk from the cavesson as he tried to head out up the paddock. The jolt slowed him down. He felt unsure. He didn't want to hurt himself, he only wanted to show this man who was boss. He shook his head twice, trying to rid himself of the cavesson: then, in answer to the calmly repeated command, he trotted forward once more in the circle. Marny gradually uncurled herself and found her position back in the saddle, her heart beating wildly and her hands trembling as she folded her arms in front of her.

In another ten minutes both Casanova and Marny had settled down. Sweat lay in a damp patch on the horse's neck as Tibor brought him back to a halt, carefully looping in the lunge-rein. Peter, watching the way he handled the lunge, was reminded of a combination of ballet dancer and matador—Months later, Tibor told them that when he was a young pupil at the Spanish Riding School, he had had to study for two years before he was allowed to work horses on the lunge.

If Marny was hoping for some words of praise from Tibor, she was disappointed. "Walk the horse until he's dry," was all he said. "Then we'll have lunch and discuss the next week's programme." As he walked away from them, they noticed that his limp seemed more pronounced than it had been earlier.

"Do you think he's too tired, Peter?" Marny asked anxiously. "I'm feeling pretty whacked myself, and after all, he's an old man."

"No, I don't," replied Peter. "You know I had a bad fall four years ago. It's much better now, but I sometimes limp when I do a lot. Probably he has an old war wound which gets worse after any strain." Then he added thoughtfully, "If I hadn't fallen off Cantrece we might never have met. Isn't that odd?"

They started walking slowly back to the house and Peter went on, "I promised myself I'd never touch another horse. I guess Szechy did too. But here we are. Marny, you're a witch."

"Don't be silly!"

"You are. The witch on horseback."

Marny laughed. "O.K. Have it your way. It does seem rather magic though, us being friends. I've never had a close friend who was a boy before."

"You've never let one be your friend. There are plenty who'd like to try. But I'm glad to be the first. Look, hurry up, the master's waiting."

Chapter 13

Peter came into the cottage, looking pleased. "I've loaded both horses back on to the float," he said. "Cas is as quiet as a lamb in there, eating his lunch with Moonie."

Tibor said seriously, "Don't under-estimate that horse."

"But he's easy to handle now," exclaimed Peter. "Surely you don't agree with Shooter—that he's got a vicious streak?"

"No," said Tibor slowly, "I don't. But that does not mean there are no problems. Casanova has *learnt* to distrust men. This has made him vicious. Another type of horse would have reacted differently—become cowed or submissive."

Marny remembered the brutal battle between Cas and Alex Shooter. "Could he *really* kill someone?" she asked.

"Yes, I'm afraid so. He could try—if he hated or feared them enough."

Marny shivered, and Peter's pleased grin faded.

"You must not dwell upon this too much, Marianne. Already the horse trusts *you*. We shall work together, increasing this trust until he reacts favourably to everyone."

"Can we do that?" Peter asked.

Tibor smiled warmly at them both. "Yes, I think so. Marianne already has achieved much. You, Peter, also have the knack with horses."

"Maybe," Peter said. "As long as I don't have to ride them."

Marny brought one of the two silver-framed photographs down from the mantelpiece and studied it intently. "Goodness," she said without thinking. "I can hardly recognise you." The words were scarcely out of her mouth before she realised how rude that must sound. She blushed furiously as Tibor gave an ironic little bow.

"Yes indeed. Somewhat of a change since those days."

"It's just that you were wearing army uniform," Marny said confusedly, hating herself.

"What a splendid horse," said Peter. The photograph showed a mare standing perfectly balanced, looking ready to execute any command given by the slim, erect rider on her back.

"That's Capriole," Tibor told them. "She was a German-bred horse, a Hanoverian, but she had the big heart of a Hungarian. Nothing I ever asked her to perform was too much for her. I have never known such a jumper. At Rome in 1932....big fences, all nearly two metres high, and she cleared them like a bird. There was mud and slush everywhere—it had been pouring with rain, you know—but nothing worried my Capriole. She was a horse in a lifetime—a good mare, a good mare...." He lapsed into silence, letting his thoughts flow inwards. His face was very sad.

Marny picked up the second photograph. It was also of Tibor, this time mounted on a Lipizzaner stallion. The horse was balanced on his haunches, his forefeet neatly tucked under his body.

Tibor forced himself away from his memories and smiled. "That is Kaspar," he said. "He is performing the levade."

"Wasn't Cas doing that in the lesson today?" Marny asked.

"In a way," I explained the master. "But Cas executed the movement as an act of disobedience. The haute école horse performs to command. All the movements are those a horse at liberty would perform by himself."

"I never learnt any dressage before I came to you," Marny said. "The riders at home claim it's a waste of time." She was too polite to repeat Alex Shooter's rude remarks about horses performing fancy tricks like circus animals.

"I would agree with them that advanced dressage is not necessary for the average horse," said Tibor. "But," he added, "elementary dressage is essential for every riding horse, whether his work is hacking or polo or jumping. The basic training *must* be the same."

94

Marny didn't want to argue with the master, but she broke in, saying, "What about Sure Smile? She never had proper dressage training, but she always went beautifully."

"Let me explain it to you this way, Marianne. Suppose you can play the piano by ear. You'd make a nice music. But once you can read the notes and have been trained in technique, your performance *must* be better than that of the untrained performer. I'm sorry I never saw your mare. She probably had excellent natural movement. But it would still have been improved by basic dressage."

Marny nodded.

"Casanova has been trained for racing without any proper foundation. He too is a beautiful natural mover. But we will teach him to use *all* his strength to our advantage."

"It's very exciting, isn't it?" said Marny.

"No," replied Tibor, curtly. "I do *not* want you to think so. Training is arduous and often disappointing."

But Marny was glowing. She couldn't imagine how training with this master could not be thrilling.

"Sit down," Tibor told Marny, who had got up and was wandering around the room. "I want to tell you the two golden rules for successful equitation. They are easy to remember." He sat in the armchair and lit his pipe. "I wish we could speak in Hungarian or German: the English is so hard. But I will do my best. Now listen. The first rule is *Forward and straight.*"

Marny looked puzzled. "I will explain you," said the master. "Forward" means that the horse must go actively and energetically forward at all paces and in a straight line from poll to tail."

"If the horse goes forward he can't play up, can he?" Peter put in.

"Correct. You saw today that each time Casanova wanted to disobey, he must stand still to rear. To go straight is difficult for a horse, because he naturally has one side of his body stiffer than the other. We train him to develop both sides equally."

Marny thought she understood. "What's the second rule?"

"The second rule is *Your line and your speed.* Once the horse goes forward, you must keep him on the exact line that you wish to travel." Tibor rose from his armchair and began to pace the little room, dragging his lame leg. "You see....straight line....corner to corner. Think about it for a minute. How often does the horse go where *he* wants—not where the rider tells him to? No, I don't mean bolting back to the stable—though that happens too often also. 'Your line' means that you *must* ride on the exact centimetre you wish. How often do you?"

"Not very often," Marny said ruefully, adding, "If the horse doesn't go 'forward and straight' he can't keep to the 'line' anyway."

"Good. You understand the theory quickly. 'Your speed' is easy. Often we are seeing the horses either rushing or dawdling. Either way, they are keeping *their* speed, not the rider's. So remember: 'Forward and straight' and 'Your line and your speed,' and you have an instant guide in any situation."

Peter and Marny were silent, thinking about the master's words. Peter thought, "If I had had a teacher like this I'd never have had any accident."

Marny said aloud, "I don't know very much, Mr. Szechy."

"Don't be ashamed of inexperience," he replied, "if only you have the humility to learn."

"How many years did you study horse training, sir?" asked Peter.

"For more years than you are old, Peter. But a horsemaster does not stop learning until he dies." The old man started frying steaks for lunch, speaking with his back to them—almost as though he were thinking aloud. "It is strange how the thread of one life unravels and intertwines with others. If you had not seen the old photograph of me....more than twenty years, I've been away from horses—you were not even born when I stopped riding, Marianne. And yet....here we are." Marny guessed that Tibor was recalling his early life and she wished that she could share his memories: wind rustling over the vast steppes; enormous herds of mares and foals running half-wild; sleigh bells jingling in the frozen winter.

"I was born in Hungary," said Tibor, "in the days when horses were as important as cars are now. My parents owned a stud farm where we bred horses for the cavalry. Then the first World War came. During the war, horses were used, thousands of them.

Our whole stud was requisitioned. My parents stayed in Debrecen looking after the few animals that were left. The war ended, and we planned to start the stud again, this time without my two elder brothers. I had been too young to fight; they had been killed.

"It was not all misfortune. I married and we rebuilt the stud. My wife, Lise, was a good rider. You look a little like her, Marianne. We had an adopted son, Pisti, but no other children.

"Then I became interested in the work of the Italian, Caprilli."

"I know about him," Marny interrupted. "He invented the forward jumping seat."

"Exactly," Tibor smiled. He placed the sizzling steaks on the table and they began to eat. "It took a long time for Caprilli's ideas to be accepted all over Europe. When I first learned to ride, we jumped leaning backwards. Poor horses! But I was an early convert to his methods, and I selected and trained jumpers. There was some small success."

"Small!" exclaimed Marny. "That book I read says that you were European champion twice, and an Olympic gold medallist."

"Yes." Tibor seemed embarrassed. "But it is a long time since I have concentrated on jumping. Dressage became my greater love." He pointed with his fork to the photo of Kaspar. "My father sent me to the Spanish Riding School for five years."

"The dancing white horses," murmured Marny.

"Life in Vienna before the second World War," he smiled at Marny. "It was gay, especially for pretty girls like you. But later on...." He fell silent, remembering the terrible years. The war. His return to Hungary. His parents' death. The stud disbanded again, and the remaining animals taken away for war work. Lise had been shot by the enemy. He had been conscripted and injured in battle, his leg smashed by machine-gun fire. After the Communists took over in Hungary he, Tibor, had lost the will to struggle, or to rebuild the twice disbanded stud. He had escaped alone to Australia and tried to forget his past. Now it came back to him—brought by a young girl and her wild horse.

"It was all so long ago, my dear. I lost my Capriole during those years."

97

"*Lost* her?" exclaimed Marny. "But how?"

"It was the war," said Tibor simply. "After Capriole had won her jumping titles we retired her to our stud. We hoped to produce some beautiful and talented foals from her. They would carry on her tradition and bloodlines. We never did get a foal." His voice faded away almost to nothing. "Capriole was requisitioned during the war. She was too old for the mounted troops, so she was given the job of pulling cannons. She dragged those heavy things with the strength of two horses. I heard that she was shot and died instantly. A fitting end for such a courageous mare."

Marny and Peter were silent after Tibor had finished speaking. Words seemed unnecessary. The old clock on the mantelpiece ticked away slowly, then chimed the half hour. Finally, in an effort to rouse the master from his sad memories, Marny said, "My dad was hurt in the war." Why is it that things turn out so unfairly? she thought. Sigi could not be a surgeon any more than Tibor could ride; and Tibor had no child to pass his knowledge on to. She wondered what had happened to his adopted son but couldn't ask. Was that the reason he had decided to cut himself off from horses?

"Like Peter," she thought, "and me too, I suppose. If I hadn't had my family, maybe I would still be grieving for Sure Smile." For the first time, as she looked into the old man's sad, deep-set brown eyes, she realised fully how much he had lost.

"I should like to meet your father one day, Marianne. I have lived too long alone with memories."

"He would love to meet you, too. We're all so grateful to you."

"Perhaps it is I who should be grateful to you."

In the float, Casanova and Moonlight were munching hay; and Ugly Duckling, gorged on rats from Tibor's grain store, was asleep. Marny ached all over from lack of sleep, the strain of the lesson, and all she had learnt in one short day.

She said drowsily to Peter, " 'S wonderful."

"What is?"

"You is. He is. Cas is." She fell fast asleep. Peter stopped to tuck a rug around her and drove home smiling, thinking of his father. "Cunning old so-and-so. He guessed all along about Marny and me—before I did myself. Wonder if he'll be right about riding too?" He gave Marny a squeeze.

"Mm. Yes. *Forward and straight,*" she muttered, without waking up.

Chapter 14

Candida laughed. "I'd love to chaperone you and Cas along the Armidale roads."

"Thanks, Candy, you're wonderful. Can we make it Tuesdays and Fridays? No, we can't: you won't have any free afternoons left then."

"It doesn't matter. Variety is the spice of life, they tell me. So long as I don't have to get up with you at six to feed him."

"You won't. 'Bye." Marny hung up and let out a joyful yell.

"What's happening?" Sigi rushed from his study, alarmed. "Have you hurt yourself, Marianne?"

"Course not, Dad. I'm just happy." She kissed the top of her father's head and pranced out of the room to find Trudy and tell her all the wonderful things that were happening.

The week flew by. Every day after school the two girls took Moonlight and Casanova out on quiet hacks to accustom Cas to traffic and strange sights, and early every morning, after her stable duties were completed, Marny carried out Tibor's training programme in the small paddock. By Saturday, she thought the master ought to be full of praise for her week-long efforts.

The next lesson at Tibor's farm started with the usual twenty-minute lunging session. Then Tibor gave her a leg-up. "Walk around for a few minutes on a loose rein, Marianne. Remember—guide him with your legs, not your hands. Inside leg on the girth; outside leg behind the girth for every turn. He must learn to follow this direction without the use of the reins." Marny knew what her instructor wanted—it was a basic concept she understood from her books on equitation.

She urged Casanova forward, the reins hanging loose. His head was stretched down, low and relaxed. By now he was beginning to understand these new aids. When he could not interpret her leg signals, Marny helped him out by showing the direction with a slight pressure on the relevant rein.

"Take up the contact with the reins gradually so that you don't interfere with the rhythm of the walk," commanded Tibor. Marny obeyed, but she did not push sufficiently with her legs, and Casanova broke rhythm and slowed down. Tibor noticed immediately. "Let him out at a free walk and start again." The second attempt was successful, and Cas proceeded round the field at an ordinary walk, the reins lightly taut, his stride long and free. "Trot on," Tibor commanded. As the pace increased, Marny automatically "gave" with the reins so that they looped like spaghetti.

"Come in to me," Tibor ordered.

What had she done wrong? Her legs hurt from constant pushing, and her head ached from intense concentration. "Hopeless," she thought miserably. "Why *did* I think I could ride?" Oh, for the carefree days at Shooter's, when everyone had praised her horsemanship. By present standards she couldn't even trot properly.

Tibor observed her glum expression and said gently, "The reins are like the lunge-line. Keep contact *all* the time, unless you are riding on a loose rein. Then you must let the reins go completely slack—not just a little looped. Remember: keep your wrists rounded and your fingers closed on the reins." Marny's head drooped sadly. "Come now, I told you how hard it would be."

Marny looked into Tibor's dark eyes and she saw with what assurance he stood in the centre of the circle, erect despite his lame leg. None of the praise she had known in the Sure Smile days would be showered over her here, but what they were working towards today was something much finer than any quick success or a prize in a show.

"Sorry." She straightened up and paid attention.

"Think of the reins as a pair of doves," said Tibor, "that you neither want to harm nor can allow to fly away." Marny glanced down at her hands. She'd been allowing the reins to slide through her fingers like a greasy rope.

"Try again," commanded the master.

Marny urged Casanova forward into an active trot. She attempted to keep her wrists supple and to give and take with the movements of the trot without allowing the reins to slip. She did not succeed all the time, but Tibor knew how far to push her. He made no comment. After working them first on the right and then on the left rein he called out, "Loose rein!"

Marny slowed to a walk and then let her reins go.

"No, no!" cried Tibor. "At the trot!" Marny sent the horse forward again, but as she lengthened the rein, Cas began to increase his pace until he was cantering—an ugly, sprawling canter. Marny had to bring him back to a trot once more.

"Steady, Cas," she whispered. "Please be good! I'm sure the lesson is nearly over."

Eight times Marny loosened the reins, and eight times Casanova rushed forward. Finally he realised what his rider wanted: he could relax and stretch his neck out; he wasn't expected to tear off as soon as the reins slackened. He felt relieved, for he was getting tired too.

"At last!" sighed Marny as, on her ninth attempt, Casanova did not alter pace but continued his steady trot, his head and neck stretching down.

"Good!" was the master's comment. "Now try the exercise on the other rein." This time Casanova understood. He behaved perfectly.

"That's enough for today," Tibor said at last. Marny gratefully halted Casanova and vaulted off. She ran her stirrups up while Peter loosened the girth. Tibor said nothing about their progress, but Marny sensed he was pleased.

This weekend, Marny had brought a picnic lunch for the three of them to share. As they ate, they talked quietly together like people who had been friends for a long time. Marny found that when she was with Peter and Tibor Szechy, her shyness left her.

103

Tibor told them stories of his days in the cavalry. "There was one captain," he said, "who was very unpopular. He was always bragging about his riding ability. He wasn't especially good, but he always bought superb chargers, and even an indifferent rider would have put up a show on the magnificent animals he owned. One day, one of us bet him that he couldn't ride a certain known quiet horse. If he couldn't he would have to buy all the officers a champagne dinner. He agreed and we all came to watch the challenge. The horse was led out. He was a flea-bitten grey. The captain vaulted on. The moment he was up the grey began to buck, and within seconds the captain was off. Unfortunately, the trial was held on a very muddy bit of ground, and he was covered in mud. We all claimed our bet at once and he had to take us out to dinner covered in mud from head to foot."

"Why did the horse buck?"

"Well—mm—I'm not quite sure. You see, the captain didn't check his girth before he mounted. I imagine someone *might* have placed something like a burr under the girth."

"Who would have done that?"

"I don't know," said Tibor, with a glint of mischief in his eyes, "but we had a fine champagne dinner."

Marny and Peter spent so long chatting to Tibor that it began to grow late. Leaving Casanova at the farm in readiness for tomorrow's lesson, they headed off for Armidale, hoping to reach home before dusk.

"I've never drunk champagne," said Marny, as the blue utility sped along through the lengthening shadows.

Peter looked at her sideways. "I haven't got any champagne, but how would you like to go to a dance?"

Marny looked puzzled. "The university ball is on at the end of term. I'm taking you."

"Peter, don't be silly. What would I wear?"

"I don't know—what *do* girls wear? You're not Cinderella, are you? Trudy'll have some ideas."

"O.K.," laughed Marny. "I'd love to come."

Trudy was far more thrilled than her daughter at the prospect of the ball. On Monday morning she prepared to rush off to the shops to buy fabric and a pattern.

"You're impossible, Marny. Your first ball and you won't even come and choose the material for the frock."

"I'm sorry, Mum. Please understand. I can't let up on Cas's training even for a day. Besides, you know what suits me."

"Oh, mothers never understand," Trudy grumbled. When she returned from her shopping spree, she rang up Janey Thomas, Candida's mother, for a comforting moan about teenage daughters.

"You can't have it both ways," Janey said unsympathetically. "Candy's been nagging for weeks for a black velvet evening cloak as well as her dress."

Candy could talk about nothing but clothes when she and Marny set out for their hack on Tuesday. It seemed everyone they knew would be going to the end-of-term ball. The girls rode past the railway yards (empty of horses today) and into the town's stock reserve, where they had sixteen hectares of undulating country to explore. Casanova seemed nervous, shying at bits of paper and trembling at the rustling of the gumleaves. Marny could feel his heart pounding beneath her legs. Moonlight was calm as ever: he was a marvellous schoolmaster. Candida knew that he talked to the nervous Thoroughbred, explaining that it was only paper, shadows, and leaves that frightened him, and that the long smoking dragon was only a goods train which would never attack an innocent horse.

"I couldn't manage these rides without you," Marny told her friend gratefully.

"Don't thank me, thank Moonlight."

"Thank you, Moonlight." She leant across to pat the cob's thick neck. As she did so, the trailing silk scarf Candida was wearing worked itself loose and fluttered away towards the railway lines. There was a sharp east wind blowing.

"I'll go for it," said Candida." You'd better not take Cas so near to the line. He's nervous enough today." She trotted off after her scarf and Marny continued to ride slowly down the dirt track.

A few seconds later, an old man cycled past. Balanced across the handlebars of his bicycle he carried a long iron-tipped stick. He was a council worker whose job was spearing up rubbish in the municipal parks. Casanova was wary and started to jog. Maybe nothing would have happened if the old man had not picked up speed just as a passing train gave a loud whistle. Casanova heard the sound of the dragon, and at the same time felt an iron stick graze his shoulder. Danger! He whirled around to face it, snorting with fear.

"Gerroff!" screeched the old man, terrifying the horse even more. Marny reacted fast. Before Cas could begin a bout of rearing, she urged him forward into a gallop and tore past the astonished cyclist. He wobbled and crashed off his bike, which slithered across the track and fell down the railway embankment. By the time the old man had staggered to his feet, Casanova had completely recovered from his fright and was cantering gaily back towards him. Marny reined in and dismounted to apologise.

"That damn 'orse nearly killed me!" cried the old man, his face a nasty shade of green.

"That's not true!" said Marny, hotly. "You rode far too close and scared him. Look! His shoulder's grazed."

"*His* shoulder. To hell with *his* shoulder. What about me bike?" He dragged it up the embankment and examined its bent front wheel.

Candida returned and quickly sized up the situation. Marny was too upset to calm the injured cyclist and was making matters worse.

"We are very sorry, sir," said Candida, smiling sweetly at him. "It won't happen again."

"Damn sure it won't," whined the old man. "Who's gunna pay for the damages?" He continued to complain, then insisted on taking their names and addresses. "You 'aven't heard the last of this, young ladies," he muttered angrily as he limped away, wheeling the damaged bike.

"Don't worry, Marny," Candida advised. "It was mostly his fault. Silly old man. He frightened Cas by cycling right under his nose. I think we should forget it."

"All right," said Marny in a subdued voice. "I'll try. But that old man looked so spiteful. D'you think he'll try to do anything to Cas?"

"He can't," said Candida. "We know what happened."

106

Cas made up for his earlier misbehaviour by walking home quietly, and by the time she had stabled him and had her tea, Marny had forgotten the old man's warning. Trudy had been sewing all day and wanted her to try on her new frock.

Chapter 15

Marny began to grow excited as Friday approached. She caught the feeling from Trudy, who was re-living her own youth through her daughter. Trudy loved Peter's old-fashioned manners, and now that he'd invited Marny to a ball she liked him even more. For a ball was something Trudy understood—from the invitation to the final dab of perfume behind the ears.

On the night, Candida came around to get dressed at Marny's home, where there would be no younger brothers and sisters interfering.

"You see the disadvantages in being the oldest child," she said, as she went into the bathroom to start running a luxurious bubble bath.

"You aren't going to ride tonight!" Trudy exclaimed as Marny gulped her tea and started to pull on her boots.

"Yes, I must and I want to. We're still going to Glen Innes tomorrow."

Candida heard the argument and poked her head round the bathroom door. "You ought to marry that horse," she called, unhelpfully.

"What, a gelding?" cried Marny.

"Don't be so unladylike, girls," said Trudy, pretending to be shocked.

But Marny had her way and gave Cas his hour-long lesson in the August dusk. The days were lengthening, and the fruit trees were already in blossom. The rays of the dying sun caught the sheen on Casanova's chestnut coat. His muscled neck arched proudly as he increased and decreased pace to command. He had already learnt to halt beautifully, standing squarely with his ears pricked forward. The hour passed quickly, as time always does when you are happy and occupied; then Marny went up to the house to find Candida still in her bath and Trudy beginning to flap.

"Oh, darling," she complained, "I wanted you to dress properly, not throw on your jeans in two minutes."

"I'm not wearing my jeans," said Marny in a reasonable tone.

"Well, it would not surprise me if you did," said Sigi crossly.

"Sorry, Dad," said Marny. She could see that her father had had a hard day, and knew how much he hated upsets in the house. She ran into her bedroom to change.

Marny dressed quickly and was ready at the same time as Candida. As the two girls entered his study Sigismund stood up, staring in astonishment at his little daughter (who topped him by ten centimetres).

"Come off it, Dad," she said as Sigi took her hand to kiss.

"When you look like a lady, act like one—accept compliments," he said sternly.

"O.K., I'll try," she said nervously.

"Then don't say 'O.K.' "

Trudy, who had already seen the girls dressed up in their new frocks, ushered Peter and Barry into the study with a very grand air and a proud smile. Dark, plump little Candida looked even prettier than usual in a frock of soft blue material, and Marny wore a long-sleeved velvet dress of jade green which deepened the green of her eyes. She looked very tall and quite beautiful.

"You're lovely, Marny," said Peter.

"She really is," agreed Candida happily.

It was amazing the number of people who apparently went to end-of-term dances. Hundreds of cars, motorbikes and vans choked the parking lots and surrounding roads. The sound of the band streamed out of the Madwich Hall to greet them.

Marny was self-conscious about her dancing, but found that with so many people bumping and shoving her lack of experience didn't matter.

110

"Forgot something," she yelled across at Peter.

"What?"

"How nice you look," she yelled, even more loudly.

"You don't tell boys that!" he shouted back. "You mustn't let a soul know how handsome I am!"

"If you say so!" The music drowned her words and she just danced.

The ball warmed up, with yells and whoops, balloons popping, and streamers tangling into everyone's clothes. The boys jealously guarded two enormous balloons from pins, but they burst before supper when a girl dressed in bright pink put her lighted cigarette against them.

"Oh, sorry," she said sweetly.

"Doesn't matter," said Candida, equally sweetly. It was Alice Shooter, with several of her hangers-on trailing along behind her. Marny and Peter didn't even notice her. "That's her real punishment," Candida whispered to Barry.

Blair was dancing with Jeanie McPherson, who cast a pitying look at Marny as they passed. Why on earth had she let Blair go for that stuck-up Peter Cooke-Finch? But Marny didn't notice her either. She and Peter got up and drifted away together on to the dance floor.

"Don't they look sort of—one?" said Candida.

Peter was saying to Marny, "Think we ought to go?"

"I suppose so. I can't really yawn and tell Tibor I've been dancing all night."

"I don't see why not. I'll bet he had plenty of good times when he was young." Peter glanced around the crowded noisy hall. "Let's leave now anyway, while things are still swinging."

Neither spoke very much during the drive back to Marny's home. When they reached the front gate and got out of the car, Peter took her hand and they walked up the path towards the house with its welcoming light. Marny, suddenly made self-conscious by the situation, began to chatter nervously as they reached the door, and Peter let her—until she ran out of words. Then he leaned forward and gently kissed her on the lips.

"Bye, Marny," he said. "See you tomorrow."

111

Marny went inside and tiptoed down the hall to her bedroom. Before she undressed she looked at the tall, green-eyed girl in the mirror and smiled widely. The girl in the mirror smiled back at her.

Cas improved rapidly during the following month. He grew so relaxed that Marny was often lulled into a false sense of security which was occasionally shattered by a squeal and a buck in response to the sudden noise of a truck horn or a dog barking. She felt the increasing regularity of his stride and found that it was becoming automatic to her to count the beat to each one. Tibor advised her to sing while she rode to keep the rhythm, and she found that Cas seemed to enjoy marches best at the trot and the "Blue Danube" waltz for the three-beat canter. Pedestrians gave them curious looks as they rode past, Marny singing loudly, but she didn't mind.

When Mark Thomas arrived to give Cas his second drench for worms, he commented on how fit both horse and rider looked. Tibor was increasing the difficulty of their work programme, but so imperceptibly that they hardly noticed how much more he was demanding from them. They were both developing muscle and stamina.

"How does he behave?" asked Mark, admiring the tall chestnut.

"Perfectly in the stable now, but he's still temperamental on rides."

"He's beginning to look like a stallion, with that crest on him," said Mark, fondling the horse's torn ear, a reminder of less happy days. "He's been gelded properly," he continued, "but I was wondering whether he mightn't be partly a stallion. Do you know what a rig is?"

"I think so," replied Marny, trying to remember her biology. She knew that in a male mammal the testicles develop in the abdomen and descend to their final resting-place in the scrotum in early maturity.

"What I think has happened with Cas," said Mark, "is that one testicle never descended, so that when he was gelded, he kept some stallion characteristics."

"Aren't rigs supposed to be more unreliable than stallions?"

"They are. If he *is* one, it would certainly explain his savage behaviour."

"But Mark, he's fine now."

Mark laughed at Marny's immediate defence of her horse. "She really does love that animal," he thought.

"Can't we find out?" she asked. "Cas is such a mystery horse. We know so little about him."

Mark mentioned an article he'd read recently in the *Australian Veterinary Journal*. "There's a new method of analysing urine to estimate the quantity of ketosteroids."

"Never heard of them!"

"Can't say I had much either, before I read this article, but they're present in the urine of stallions and rigs. I'll find out if Metcalfs up at the diagnostic laboratory will do the test and let you know."

Marny returned Casanova to his box and stroked his soft nose. "Why are you so beautiful?" she asked him. In reply Cas rubbed his forehead hard against her shoulder.

The Mann family usually had a late supper on Sundays when Marny and Peter brought Cas back from Glen Innes. They had just finished their coffee on this particular evening when Alex Shooter arrived looking tense and angry, stamping his dusty boots on Trudy's polished floor.

"No, I won't sit down, Mrs. Mann. What I've got to say is better said standing."

Peter put his arm protectively around Marny's shoulder.

"You can stay, young man, to hear this. You're mixed up in it too, I know."

"What *is* all this about, Mr. Shooter?" asked Trudy, impatiently. She leaned down to grasp Whisky's collar, for the normally friendly dog was growling ferociously.

"I suppose you haven't heard the name Bob Kinsey?"

"I'm sorry. It doesn't mean a thing to us."

"It will," said Shooter, grimly." Poor old Bob was damn near killed by your vicious brute."

Marny gasped, recalling the old man who had fallen off his pushbike. "I know who he means, Dad. I'd forgotten all about him." She quickly told her parents the whole story.

"The girls do not seem to be at fault, Mr. Shooter," said Sigi.

"Oh, aren't they? I suppose you don't know old Bob had a heart attack that same night—brought on by your mad antics? He's in hospital now. *And* he blames you. That horse'll have to go," he said, nastily.

"I don't see how Mr. Kinsey's health is your concern," Sigi said.

"Oh, you don't? Just let me tell you that old Bob was my father-in-law—before my poor wife died."

"I see. Well, I'm sorry your relative is ill. But I do not think Marny or her horse can be blamed. I've heard what Marny has to say, and I believe her. The horse stays."

Alex grew so red with rage that his face seemed about to pop like a blown-up paper bag. "We'll see about *that*. There's a way to force you. We're getting up a petition, and we've got hundreds of signatures already. That horse is well-known in Armidale. Next time he'll go for a kiddie."

"It's true," Marny thought miserably. Cas *was* well known. Lots of people had seen him at Shooter's when he was really savage, and anyone who didn't understand horses could easily be persuaded that his temperamental displays out on rides were dangerous.

"I've warned you. For the second time." And Alex left, slamming the door and refusing to say goodbye.

"Dad, why does he hate us so?" asked Marny, her eyes brimming with tears.

"I am afraid he is jealous, *Liebchen*. He couldn't tame the horse himself and I wouldn't sell him. We ought to pity him. I think he's been drinking again."

Peter laughed. "What harm can he do? He's just jealous—"

"Don't be callow, Peter," said Sigi sternly. "You're missing the point. Alex is well known in Armidale. People respect him. He can make a lot of trouble."

"I'm sorry, sir," said Peter. "I wasn't thinking. I just hated to see Marny upset. I could ask my dad for help. He's on the local council."

"Leave that for the time being. I want to come with you to Mr. Szechy's next weekend. I've not met him yet. Let's hear what he has to say."

114

That night Marny's dreams were fearful ones—dark and menacing. In the daytime she pushed them from her mind. How could anyone wish to harm her beautiful horse?

Tibor immediately sensed that something was wrong when the blue utility arrived with Sigi squeezed into the front seat. After Marny had unloaded Cas he told Peter to lunge the horse.

"D'you think I can do it properly?"

"You have been watching for enough weeks." Peter and Marny went to the paddock to start work and Tibor led Sigi indoors to talk. After Sigi had finished telling Tibor about the petition he added, "I don't like to worry Marny, but you'll understand. I'm a foreigner in Armidale. We're accepted now, well-liked I think, but Alex can stir up a lot of ill-feeling against us. He'll do it, too—if he can."

Tibor nodded. He made no comment on Sigi's story but said, "Doctor Mann, your daughter....is it luck or fate? I don't know....Your daughter has got hold of a remarkable horse. I am not boasting to tell you I have known many horses...."

"Of course," Sigi interrupted. "I know about you."

"Not about me, Doctor Mann. I am talking about Marny. Marny and Casanova. When they first came to me I was not sure whether Marny had the qualities necessary to ride him. Now I know." Tibor took Sigi by the arm and led him outside. "Will you walk down to the paddock and watch the training session? Then you will know better than my words can tell you."

Sigi was ignorant of the finer points of riding, but even to his inexperienced eye the change in Marny and Casanova was startling. Marny sat deep and quiet in the saddle, her aids invisible to anyone but Casanova. His stride was long and regular.

"Look at his tail!" Sigi exclaimed. "It used to be tucked between his legs, and now he's carrying it high—like a banner."

"A good observation, Doctor Mann." The master smiled. "When training was started, the horse was stiff and tense so he contracted his back muscles. Now he relaxes, and you see the difference. Tail carriage is a good indication of the state the training has reached."

"He certainly looks relaxed and free."

"Take away a horse's liberty and you'll produce an automaton."

"I can see what you mean about my daughter," Sigi replied, watching Marny make Cas flow into a canter. "But we haven't solved the problem of the petition. What I want is for you to put Cas in for some shows. Let him prove himself. Nothing convinces people like success."

"They are not ready yet. I don't wish to hurry such a fiery horse, and Marny herself seems to have lost the will to compete."

"That's all very well," said Sigi. "You know what happened at her last show. She can never forget that. But she can't live in the past any more than we can. The town is up in arms against Casanova. He's costing me a lot of money and there are no results."

Tibor sighed. "We can try."

Sigi said quickly, "Mark Thomas mentioned a One Day Event at Europambla in January. Couldn't they have a shot at it?"

Tibor reluctantly nodded agreement. But as he watched Marny and Casanova trotting figure eights, so gracefully that it seemed as if they were flowing together, he felt his gloomy thoughts disperse.

"Maybe," he thought. "Maybe."

Chapter 16

"Tibor won't want to go on with the training if there's so much bad feeling against us," Marny told Peter as they drove up to Glen Innes the following weekend. Peter nodded, looking depressed. He had telephoned his father during the week, but Charles Cooke-Finch hadn't any new ideas on how to defeat Alex Shooter's petition. "The horse will have to prove himself somehow," he had said. "You know what small towns are like. Once anything or anyone has a bad reputation it sticks." Charles had vetoed any suggestion of a counter-petition. "Only Marny's friends would sign it," he told Peter.

Tibor was waiting at the gate as usual.

"He looks damned cheerful," said Peter glumly.

"Good morning!" Tibor said to the gloomy pair. "Unload the horse quickly. I've something to show you."

Ugly Duckling leapt out first and headed for the barn before Cas was led down the ramp, his beautiful head erect and his ears pricked forward alertly. He nickered softly to Tibor.

When they reached the training paddock, Marny stopped and gasped. It looked completely different. A whole course of show jumps had been set up and placed invitingly on the turf.

"Yes," said Tibor. "They *are* for you. It is sooner than I have wanted. But in deference to the wishes of Doctor Mann, Cas starts his jumping today."

Marny gulped, then murmured, "Oh *no*. I can't believe it. Jumps. Real jumps."

"Thank you, sir," said Peter, almost as excited as Marny.

"You would do better to thank me by saddling up that horse and shaking Marianne."

Peter obeyed and soon Marny was up, walking Casanova around the paddock.

Two weeks ago Peter and Tibor had constructed several cavalletti, and Cas had already walked, trotted, and cantered over them. Marny half-expected him to shy at the gaily-coloured jumps, but he accepted the sight of them easily. Tibor's paddock was a place where nothing bad had ever happened and he enjoyed working there. Marny spent the first ten minutes warming him up with gentle trotting and cantering on a loose rein.

"Cavalletti first. Start when you're ready." When she felt that the big horse was sufficiently relaxed and going forward easily, Marny turned him toward the first six cavalletti placed in a row, each one-and-a-half metres away from the next. Casanova trotted over them in perfect rhythm, never breaking his stride, his tail held high. Marny then turned down the other side of the paddock to canter over the two cavalletti placed three-and-a-half metres apart. He gave a little buck as he broke into the canter, but he crossed the cavalletti without faltering. "Change the rein," Tibor ordered. Marny obediently turned Cas across the diagonal of the rectangle. "Simple change of leg with six trotting strides at the centre," Tibor continued. Marny concentrated hard on trying to sit deeper in the saddle, stretching down her legs and pushing to engage Casanova's hocks further under him. She knew from Tibor's repeated instructions that the slower the pace, the more active the rider must be, and the more difficult it is to ride correctly.

"Now, boy," Marny whispered as soon as she felt that Casanova's canter stride was ready for him to break into an active trot without rushing.

"Outside rein, inside leg!" Tibor called.

"Good boy," whispered Marny, her teeth still clenched with concentration as Cas responded to her aids and, on the sixth trotting stride, broke into a canter, leading with the correct leg.

"Ho hup!" Tibor called as Marny lowered her hands on to the horse's neck, approaching the cavalletti from the opposite side.

Suddenly Casanova plunged forward, kicking his hindlegs up high and squealing, a highpitched sound which terrified the wits out of Peter, who had been quietly leaning against the paddock rails, dozing in the sun. With a terrific leap Casanova jumped the two cavalletti in one stride and proceeded to gallop around the paddock, squealing, pigrooting, and twisting from side to side. Marny, nearly dislodged at the first leap, clung on and gradually regained her seat. She was so proud of her horse's tremendous jump that she almost enjoyed his naughtiness. Cas continued to gallop, ears forward, a gleam of mischief in his eyes. This wasn't the savage animal of a few months ago but a spirited Thoroughbred full of the joy of living.

"Sorry!" Marny called out as soon as Casanova came to a halt. But Tibor was pleased. Firstly, Marny hadn't fallen off— which she surely would have done a few weeks ago. Secondly, the big horse showed jumping ability. Thirdly, and most important, Casanova was beginning to enjoy himself and play.

"Trot over the cavalletti and go round again" Tibor told his panting pupil.

This time Casanova trotted up. He broke into a canter stride over the first cavalletto, then he bounced neatly over the second as if to say, "This is too easy."

"Good," said Tibor. Marny smiled and patted Casanova's damp neck. When Tibor said "Good," she knew they'd done well.

Peter ran to help Tibor adjust the standards and cups and fit the brick wall together at its lowest height of 65 centimetres. Without being told, Marny was walking Cas around the paddock on a loose rein to cool him. She realised now that the pace of Tibor's training sessions, which seemed slow compared with the frenzied rush at Alex Shooter's, produced a calm and obedient horse who enjoyed his work and didn't need to be beaten. She thought of poor Mirabelle and sighed.

Soon the small course was arranged to Tibor's satisfaction. "Trot the cavalletti, then jump the ditch and rails from the trot."

Cas trotted over the familiar cavalletti and then Marny turned him towards the 60-centimetre ditch with the small hogsback behind it. Cas began to tense as he approached this strange object. "Forward! Ride him forward!" Tibor called out. Marny

119

obeyed and pushed the big horse energetically. No baulking for Casanova. He launched himself into the air, jumping far too high and wide for the low obstacle. As he landed he squealed and bucked twice—more from amazement at his accomplishment than anything else.

"Again," Tibor called as they trotted past. Cas repeated the enormous leap, but not the display buck. He trotted on firmly, swishing his tail with a selfsatisfied air.

"Brick wall next, after the cantering cavalletti."

Cas snorted, nostrils dilated, eyes bulging, at the red-and-white monstrosity in front of him. Marny rode him forward and straight without being reminded, and Cas jumped high, kicking up behind. Marny, unused to these gymnastics, hung on to his mane to keep her balance. Tibor waved her on to the next jumps. Cas popped over the rustic gate, then suddenly saw the parallel bars two strides ahead. He didn't want to jump twice in succession so he tried to run out, but Marny held him straight with left hand and leg, and before he realised it, he had jumped the bars with plenty to spare.

Casanova was *ready* to jump. Marny could feel it now in every muscle of his body. Schooled not to pull or to rush, he was obeying her aids automatically and was enjoying himself. She began to trot him on a loose rein, and gradually allowed him to stretch his neck and walk completely relaxed. The pattern behind Tibor's planning of every stage of this schooling became clear to her. She had wondered if they would ever start jumping after so many weeks of flat work, and now she saw how all the transitions, the shortening and lengthening of stride, had led up to this—a horse jumping, freely, boldly, and happily. She felt humble as she met the master's eyes, sure that he had read her thoughts as easily as he had guided the training.

"That will be all for today," he said quietly.

Peter and Marny drove back to Armidale a great deal more cheerfully than they had made the journey to Glen Innes.

"Isn't he incredible?" Marny said.

"Who—Cas or Tibor?"

"They both are, but I meant Tibor."

"I know. I was just teasing. It makes me feel dreadful to realise how I must have over-ridden poor Cantrece."

"I suppose it was luck with Sure Smile," Marny said. "Imagine if *she'd* had Tibor to train her."

"Let's not brood about the past, love. There are plenty of problems in the present. We still haven't solved the Shooter question."

"I know." Marny came back to earth. She had been imagining Cas at his first show. "We've got to stop Shooter's petition somehow."

"I'll try to think up something this week, Marny. Just carry on riding quietly....Don't take Cas where people will see him. At least, not for a bit."

Marny shivered. Fate had dealt her one blow, when Sure Smile had been run over. Surely she couldn't be unlucky twice?

Chapter 17

One afternoon when Marny and Candida were hacking, they met a group of Shooter horses out on a ride with Alice leading. Cas, seeing a strange group of horses, began to prance.

"Keep that animal under control, for heaven's sake," Alice scolded. "Do you want *another* accident?" Marny reddened as all the Shooter riders stared curiously at her.

"Where are you heading for, anyway?" continued Alice.

"We're riding west," answered Marny. "Thanks. I'll steer clear," said Alice rudely as she wheeled Mirabelle around, followed by her father's pupils.

Marny had tears of anger in her eyes.

"Don't be upset," Candida comforted. "She's never had any manners. It's such a lovely afternoon—let's have a long ride and forget all about her."

"But suppose the petition succeeds."

"I said *forget* it."

"O.K." said Marny, as they began to leave the houses behind and head into the bush. "Isn't it peaceful here?"

"And there are *no people,*" said Candida with feeling. For half an hour they rode in a companionable silence down a winding track which skirted the mountain. Thick bush was all around them. The path, partially overgrown and very stony, led to Barea, a ghost mining town.

"Poor Moonie. These slopes aren't too good for his rheumatism." Candida patted the cob as he struggled gamely downwards, his hind hooves skidding on the loose gravel.

"We won't take him into the mountains again," said Marny. "Though I'll miss these rides when....what was that?"

They listened carefully, but could hear nothing except the whispering sounds of the bush.

"I thought I heard something," said Marny, reining Cas in. "Listen—there it is again. It sounds like a cry."

This time Candida heard it too. "That's crazy," she said. "It's coming from down there," and she pointed away from the path down the mountain side. The tangled undergrowth ended at a little outcrop of rock about fifty metres below them. The drop was steep. They peered over the edge and called out, "Anybody down there?" This time there was no mistaking the sound of a muffled wail.

Candida leapt off Moonlight and flung the reins across to Marny. "Hang on to that. I'll go and see." Swiftly she clambered down the slope and vanished. All Marny could hear now were bird calls and the skittery sounds of loose rocks dislodged as Candida descended. Soon she came into view again, panting.

"There are two kids down there, and one of them's hurt. We'll have to bring them up somehow. They're too big to carry."

"Cas'll go down," said Marny decisively. "Moonie can't." She mounted and turned Casanova towards the steep cliff face. He hesitated at stepping off the path, but trusting Marny had become his habit, and so he obeyed the gentle, insistent pressure of her legs. Stones, dirt, and leaves were thrown up as he slipped and skidded, hind hooves beneath him, front hooves splayed out in front. Marny leant well forward and gave him his head, keeping up a soothing murmur of "Steady, steady." As the slope became steeper, Cas began to slide. Marny could hear the numerous small landslides set off from their descent. She could not control Cas, and he could not control himself. The last fifteen metres were hellish, with only the horse's powerful haunches preventing an accident. Then the ground levelled out to where two small boys were huddled beneath the overhang. Marny jumped down and ran to them. They were about eight and ten years old, and their faces were scratched and bleeding.

"How on earth did you get here?" she asked.

"Me and Tom was exploring to the ghost town and Tom fell down," replied the younger child. "I bin here with him for hours. I dunno what to do. I can't lift him." Tom was barely conscious. A large, solid boy, he had badly injured his hand and shoulders.

"You're going to be O.K.," said Marny, trying to sound reassuring. She looked upwards. It wasn't far, but it was very steep. She would have to attempt to carry the children up herself. If she left them and went back to the town it would be nightfall before they could be rescued. She was sure it would be too dangerous to leave the injured boy for so long.

"What's your name?" she asked the little one. He smiled through the streaks of dirt. "I'm Pete. Tom's me mate."

"O.K. Pete. Up you go." Without giving the boy time to become scared she legged him up on to Cas, who stepped backwards nervously.

"Cas," she whispered. "Cas, you've *got* to trust me. It's *all right*. It's all right." Cas trembled and stood still. Marny bent down and, praying for enough strength, grasped the injured Tom under his arms and slowly lifted him up till he was draped over her right shoulder. She staggered with the weight. "Over, Cas." She motioned the big horse to turn so that he was standing slightly below her, and Cas obeyed the familiar stable command. Marny was now level with his back. With Pete's help she somehow managed to heave Tom up on to the saddle. He moaned at being moved, but he was conscious enough to understand what was happening. "Hold on, boys," said Marny encouragingly.

Candida's head appeared over the edge of the rocky incline. "They're coming up!" Marny yelled. "Ho hup, Cas, hup boy!" Obediently the big chestnut turned up the slope. His hooves took purchase, and he began the climb. Marny had knotted the reins on his neck so that he was free, and she walked beside him with one arm around Tom, who was only just managing to cling on to the saddle. The boys were too surprised to be frightened, although the ascent was so steep that at several places Cas could barely keep his feet. Marny was powerless. She could only pray, "Please God, let them get up safely."

As soon as Cas reached the top of the slope, Candida caught his bridle and encouraged him to make the last effort. With one

enormous heave he breasted the slope and gained the path, panting. Sweat lay thickly on his flanks.

Candida was white-faced. From where she had been peering over the edge the ascent had looked impossible, and she had been terrified that Cas would lose his footing and fall several hundred metres into the ravine. Now that the worst was over, the two girls hugged one another.

Candida lifted Pete on to Moonlight's saddle, and the small boy suddenly began to tremble and cry from sheer relief. Tom was silent. Marny mounted behind him so that she could support him with one hand, and they began the trek back into town. Casanova's foreleg shook convulsively, but otherwise he seemed unhurt. His breathing was still rasping from the effort he had made. Marny determined that Mark Thomas should look him over as soon as possible.

Tom suddenly piped up, "What a brave horse you've got. Maybe he'll get a boy scout badge."

"Whew!" Candida grinned with relief to hear Tom speak.

"Don't talk too much, Tom," Marny warned him. "Let's get you to hospital first."

It was dark by the time they turned up the street towards the hospital with its flashing fluorescent "Outpatients" sign. Marny thought it the most beautiful sight in the world. Candida ran inside to call for help and Marny felt each of her bones begin to ache separately. She held on to Tom until Sigi Mann ran out, followed by two orderlies carrying a stretcher. Tom was taken inside and Marny fell into her father's arms. He stroked her hair and murmured gently, "Go on home, *Liebchen*. Candy has told me what happened. Go home. I'll be back when we've examined the two boys."

"I'm all right," said Pete chirpily. "It's only me mate who was hurt. I gotta get home or Dad'll skin me."

"You come inside and be examined, my lad," said Sigi. "We'll ring your parents."

A crowd had gathered outside the gate to watch this strange sight of casualties being brought into hospital on horseback. "Reminds me of the old days," said one elderly man in a weather-beaten bush hat.

As the two girls turned wearily away from the hospital to remount, a man stepped out of the crowd. "Aren't you the Mann girl?" he asked.

"Yes," Marny replied.

"Then—that must be what they call the killer horse?"

"Yes," said Marny, too tired to argue.

"Doesn't look like a killer to me," said the man. "I'd better introduce myself, Miss Mann. I'm Mike Van. I'll have to look into this. Well, goodnight to you."

"Goodnight," said Marny, and the two girls began the long walk home.

"Don't you know who Mr. Van is?" asked Candida excitedly, as soon as they were away from the crowd. "He's the editor of the Armidale Examiner. He'll publish the story of the rescue and then everyone'll know the truth about Cas!"

"I hope so," said Marny. But at that moment she felt too weary to care.

Chapter 18

Marny went to school as usual the next morning, worried about Casanova because Sigi wouldn't let her wait for the vet's visit. But rumours travel fast in a country town, and the Mann telephone rang all morning. Trudy was glad that her husband and daughter were away so that she could cope with this, and with the well-meaning and the curious who kept dropping in.

"I *am* sorry that we signed the petition," said one visitor. "Well, Mr. Shooter *said* the horse was a killer...."

"Wait until my Women's Auxiliary gets hold of Mr. Shooter," said another wrathfully.

"Don't be too hard on Alex Shooter," Trudy told them. "He's been under a lot of strain lately."

"Oh, you good kind soul," gushed the first lady. "Turning the other cheek like a true Christian." Trudy mumbled something and did her best to usher them out. Just as they were leaving and she was preparing to start her housework, a green Volkswagen drove up. Trudy re-fixed the smile on her face and prepared to start her explanations all over again.

Marny came home at four to find a crowd gathered in the sitting-room, waiting for her. The mothers of both the rescued children were there, and both kissed her at once. "What *would* have happened without this brave girl and her wonderful horse," said Mrs. Burns, Tom's mother.

"They were naughty boys to run off like that. But they're all right now." Pete's mother was happily telling the rescue story to Mrs. Rowbotham and Mr. Van of the *Armidale Examiner*. Marny made her escape, then sighed with relief to see Mark Thomas sitting quietly in the background watching the fuss. She ran anxiously up to him.

"Nothing to worry about," he smiled. "I've done a full examination. He's lost a bit of blood from lacerations, but it's nothing serious. He'll be fit again in a couple of days."

"Ah, the dear horse!" cried Mrs. Rowbotham. "Aren't we going to see him, Marny?" Marny laughed and led everyone down to the stable yard, running on ahead, to warn Casanova that visitors were coming. Cas heard her and nickered a welcome. He was looking beautifully groomed and brushed. Then a familiar voice said, "Congratulations, Marny," and a familiar figure moved forward out of the shadows.

"Peter! How did you know?"

"Your father telephoned me at university and I came on down. I've been here for hours prettying up Cas for the photographers."

But just then everyone arrived at the stable yard and Marny's confusion was covered by oohs and aahs of delight as Peter led Casanova out to be formally presented to his audience. The setting sun caught his chestnut coat in a gleam of fire.

"He looks like a racehorse," exclaimed Mr. Van, who remembered Phar Lap.

"We think he was on the track once," said Mark. Whereupon these two men retired into a corner to swap stories of racing and racehorses.

"Look at his poor leg," cried Mrs. Kirsty, Pete's mother. Casanova's leg was swathed in a gleaming white stable bandage.

"It's not serious," said Marny. "The wound's deep, but it's clean." She herself was covered in scratches.

"Ah!" said Mr. Van, suddenly. "Here's what I've been waiting for."

Tom and Pete's fathers had been to the newspaper office to await the first edition of the evening paper, and they now came into the yard with a large bundle from which they distributed copies to everyone. Marny read the story aloud:

TEENAGERS IN MOUNTAIN RESCUE

An Armidale girl and her horse yesterday rescued two injured boys at Caulders Bluff. Marianne Mann, 16, rode her chestnut gelding Casanova 50 metres down a steep slope to bring the boys to safety.

Thomas Burns, 10, and Peter Kirsty, 8, had fallen down a steep slope at the Bluff and were sheltering beneath an overhang when they were found.

Marianne Mann was riding with her friend, Candida Thomas, 17, when they heard the boys' cries. "It was a most dangerous climb," Candida Thomas said later. "The horse could easily have slipped."

Marianne Mann lifted the two boys on to Casanova and led them back to the path where her friend was waiting. They took the boys to Armidale Hospital, where Thomas Burns was treated for a broken collar bone and concussion. Both children were suffering from bruises and shock.

Marianne Mann's father, Dr Sigismund Mann, explained later that Casanova had been a "vicious stray" when they acquired him. "There has been a remarkable improvement in his character," he said.

"My daughter is now training him for competition work."

Marny put down the paper and looked around at the circle of her friends and admirers. Everyone clapped her, and Mr. Van called out: "Three cheers for Casanova!"

"I don't think we're going to hear any more about Shooter's petition," Peter whispered to her through the sound of cheering.

"I don't think so either," Marny whispered back.

They were right. Alex Shooter quietly dropped his petition when he found out about the mountain rescue. He also lost some customers at the riding school through his attitude towards Marny and her big horse. Marny soon forgot about him in the whirl of end-of-term exams and the onset of summer.

Cas became stronger and fitter and Marny had to work hard keeping the lively horse exercised. After the rescue Candida decided to retire Moonlight, and now Marny and Cas had to take their hacks by themselves. Cas might have missed Moonie's company, as Marny did Candida's, but they went faster and further without them. Sigismund was pleased with his daughter, and not only because she was so enthusiastic and happy all the time. When the end-of-term results became official, he called her into his study. She sat on the arm of his chair while he puffed on his pipe.

"We had an agreement about horses and school, Marianne. You've kept your part of the bargain."

"Thanks, Dad. You have too. But I've enjoyed doing it anyway."

"Yes," said Sigi weightily. "I stood by you and that horse when everyone was against you. I've stood up to Mr. Shooter, and I've spoken to Mr. Szechy. The plans for competing are going on. But....what about your career?"

"You know what I want, Dad."

"You aren't going to change your mind? You'd rather treat animals than people?"

"I'm afraid so."

Sigi grunted. He'd known the answer anyway. "Look in the top drawer, Marianne." She obeyed him and brought out a sheaf of forms.

"Yes, that's right," he said. "They're the application forms to study veterinary science at university next academic year."

Chapter 19

Early on Saturday morning, Peter and Marny set off for Glen Innes.

"I think we could do this trip with our eyes closed," remarked Peter.

"Be harder for the car, though," said Marny. "How did your exams go, by the way?"

"Passed, probably. I shouldn't think I've done as well as you, though. We don't get our results until Christmas Eve."

"How awful!"

"Then they come on a computer print-out."

"Ugh, I wouldn't like that! Too impersonal."

"That's modern university for you, my girl. You'll find out soon enough. Haven't you imagined what it'd be like?"

"I suppose I haven't. I never think too far ahead. I know it's a fault."

"Have you thought about where you're going to practise when you're qualified?"

"No, not really."

Peter looked at her sideways. "How about you come and work for my dad? Then I can see you every day!"

Marny laughed. "You're not serious, surely?"

"You never know," replied Peter, his face reddening slightly. "But there's plenty of time yet. And you'll have lots of exams to pass!"

"Don't I know it!"

They smiled at each other as the car turned into Tibor's gate.

Peter unloaded Cas and then went to help Tibor with the jumps. Marny noticed that his limp was better this summer in the warm sunshine. Casanova, sensitive to her wandering attention, nudged her in the small of the back.

"I love you too, boy," she told him, patting his nose. "And now it's time to work."

They began on the flat, but Marny wasn't doing very well. "Accuracy is all-important," Tibor stressed as Marny muffed a circle. "If you can ride a correct circle, the battle is half over."

"I *am* circling. I can't help it if Cas goes a few inches out." She bit her lip, wishing she hadn't spoken.

"It is purely a matter of concentration." Tibor frowned. "Dismount!"

Marny vaulted off, and Tibor took hold of the bridle. *"Now* what do I do?" asked Marny.

"Simple," said Tibor. "Run a correct circle."

"How?"

"On your own two legs."

Marny set off furiously. She made ten attempts before she ran a circle accurately enough to please the master.

"Remount and trot the same circle."

Casinova seemed impossibly tall as Marny struggled up on to his back. Only her determination not to show weakness kept her going. They circled over and over, turning, turning, turning, the big horse flexing in the direction he was moving, his whole body bent along the circumference of the circle. Marny was feeling the strain when finally Tibor said, "That will do. Now walk large on a loose rein." That meant a short respite for girl and horse until the next movement.

Next Tibor began to teach Casanova to lengthen his stride, at the trot. "This groundwork must be firm," he told Marny. "Eventually this strong trot will culminate in the extended trot."

Marny had seen this trot at a dressage class in Sydney.

"One day your horse will float in extension," Tibor promised.

"Do you hear that, boy?" Marny patted Cas's neck.

Tibor asked for the lengthening of stride across the diagonal of the roughly marked out *manége*. Old powdered milk cans indicated the corners, centre, and quarter-markers of a rectangle measuring twenty by sixty metres.

"No, no, *don't* lose contact!" he called as Marny let the reins slide through her fingers again. "As he lengthens his stride, he will lower his head and neck automatically. *Then* allow him to stretch, but *don't* lose contact. It throws him off balance."

Marny tried again, and Casanova performed some lovely strong trots across the diagonal. Peter saw how the beautiful free movement of Cas's shoulders enabled him to throw out his forelegs. His hindlegs drove powerfully under his body and his whole outline lengthened as he thrust forward, head and neck slightly lowered and outstretched.

"Loose rein now," called Tibor, obviously pleased with their work.

As the horse slowed down, Marny was conscious of a nagging pain in her side. It had started in the car on the drive up, but she had ignored it. "Mind over matter," she said aloud. Cas cocked his torn ear back at her and walked on.

The jumps were set up at 90 centimetres and 105 centimetres. Casanova had been progressing brilliantly. He loved jumping, which was done only on weekend lessons. Marny shortened her stirrups two holes and waited for Tibor's instructions.

"Take the course from the right. Jump the combination last."

She felt the surge of power beneath her as Casanova approached the rails. The uncomfortable feeling in her abdomen receded as she counted the strides and with perfect timing placed him for take-off. But as they finally cantered up to the combination, it increased a hundredfold, taking her by surprise. She collapsed against Casanova's neck, hot pain knifing through her side.

Peter cried out in alarm and ran forward. The big horse was one stride away from the jump. Receiving no commands from his inert rider, he gathered himself up and soared over, effortlessly. Marny screamed as she fell and rolled clear. Then she fainted.

Peter reached her first. As she regained consciousness, he was chafing her hands. Marny pointed mutely to her side.

"Get her to the hospital straight away," said Tibor. "It's not the fall. I thought something was wrong earlier." Carefully the

135

two men carried Marny to the car and wrapped her in a blanket. "How's Cas?" she mumbled.

"Do not worry. I shall look after him," Tibor said gently. "Will you make it to Armidale, little one?"

"I'll try," Marny moaned.

Peter drove as fast as he could and Marny remained semi-conscious most of the time. The jolting and bouncing of the car was torture. When they reached the surgery, Peter raced up the steps, pushing past the middle-aged receptionist and calling loudly for Dr. Mann. The doctor rushed out almost immediately.

"What is the matter?"

"It's Marny. She's in the back of the car."

Sigi ran outside and took a hurried look at his daughter. "Drive straight to the hospital" he told Peter. "I'll meet you there."

"What's wrong?" breathed Peter.

"I don't know yet. I think it's appendicitis."

Two hours later Marny was in the operating theatre: diagnosis—acute appendicitis. Sigi was observing the operation while Trudy and Peter waited outside. Two hours later Sigi came out of the theatre, still gowned.

"She'll be all right. We were lucky. Riding could have ruptured her appendix...." He put his arm around Trudy and looked at Peter. "Sorry, son, you had a bad time."

Peter looked at the tubby little man and smiled. The word "son" had slipped out so naturally. "It's over now, sir. When can I see her?"

"Tomorrow."

Marny woke up from the anaesthetic next morning to find her parents at her bedside. They had both spent the night keeping vigil over their only child,

"Casanova?" was her first word.

"Peter drove up to Glen Innes this morning to see about him. He'll come and tell you this afternoon what is happening," Trudy reassured her.

"But he must be worked," said Marny groggily.

"Don't worry, young lady."

"When will I be able to ride?"

"Not for five or six weeks."

Marny tried to lift up her head. What would happen to Cas's training programme now? But soon everything went hazy and she drifted back to sleep.

"What *are* we going to do?" Peter had brought the big chestnut out of Tibor's makeshift stable and stood holding him by the halter rope. Casanova sniffed the air, his eyes big and dark.

"That is no problem," Tibor replied firmly. "*You* may ride this horse."

"What, me! I haven't been on a horse for four years. I'll never ride again."

Tibor grimaced at his own stiff leg. "I also have not ridden for many years."

Peter felt ashamed. Tibor had read his thoughts, and knew that he was afraid to ride with his leg injury. But as his father had predicted, his leg was almost completely better. Tibor's injury would never improve. Peter knew that Tibor was often in pain after a training session. This showed by minute tightening of the lines around his eyes but never by any words.

"I'm not afraid," said Peter slowly. "It's only that I promised myself I'd never ride again...." He stood beside Casanova, his arm caressing the warm neck, and blurted out to Tibor the story of how he had raced his unfit mare. He told him how she had broken her back over a jump; how his own leg had been smashed; how he had promised himself never to ride another horse until, through Marny, he had become involved with Casanova. Peter had never told the story so completely even to Marny. When he had finished, he waited for Tibor's comments, not knowing what sort of reaction to expect from him. But the old man said nothing. He brought out Casanova's tack and saddled up without a word.

"You must ride Casanova," he said finally. Peter turned to mount; he was very pale. "I regret forcing you. If I could ride myself, I would." He swung his injured leg forward. It would never bend enough to enable him to mount.

"Mount, Peter. You are fortunate that you can."

Peter thought, "How could I have been so callous? How wretched for him, seeing me too scared to try again when he can't—not ever." He placed his hands across the saddle, and as if by magic his muscles seemed to remember what to do. He vaulted lightly on to the horse's back. Cas side-stepped, alarmed by the unfamiliar presence.

"Relax," said Tibor as Peter tightened the reins in response to the horse's uneasiness. "Be careful. He knows a strange rider."

Indeed Casanova did. No man had been astride him since Alex Shooter's failure. He pawed the ground impatiently. The weight of a man on his back brought back memories.

On the racetrack the turf is emerald green, and pink pots of geraniums flank the grandstands. Crowds of people push and strain, staring at him and the other aristocrats parading in the stewards' enclosure before the race. The bandy-legged jockeys are astride their mounts: they are dressed in coloured silks and each carries his short whip. He is the biggest colt in the ring. But he does not like his own jockey—he fears him.

The crowd gasps as the colt rears, made impatient by the strapper's too-tight hold on his bridle, and flashes his baby teeth. All the way to the starting stalls he pulls and strikes out at any horse unwise enough to approach him. He hears the subdued murmur of the crowd and feels the tension in the air. He hates it all. At last he stands trembling in his starting box, ears flattened, tail twitching. The gun is fired.

Casanova gave a high-pitched scream and leapt into the air. He twisted and landed facing the other way, sides heaving, foaming at the mouth, sweat appearing in patches on his body. Peter attempted to make him walk forward.

"What the hell is the matter, Tibor?" he cried, shocked and pale with fright.

"Keep calm. Something upset him when you mounted. I think it was his memories."

Tibor caressed the horse and spoke to him until Peter felt the taut muscles relax beneath him. "Walk on," commanded the master. Cas obeyed, and strode out around the familiar, well-trodden *manège*. Tibor worked them both lightly, and Peter found he was enjoying himself more each minute. Casanova's strange behaviour had been alarming but had at least driven all thoughts of his own fears from his mind.

Casanova worked quietly. He felt the difference between his new rider and Marny. Peter was stronger. It was this strength that had reminded Cas of his jockey. But Peter also had the same instinctive "feel" that Marny had. After watching them both Tibor said, "You will be all right. Casanova has accepted you."

Peter was glad to dismount. His muscles were aching from their unaccustomed work, but he was humming cheerfully as he rubbed the gelding down and put on the stable bandages.

"I wish we knew what frightened him," he said to Tibor.

"Maybe it is better that we cannot. Horses as well as men may have bitter memories."

Chapter 20

Peter slowly climbed the steps leading to the Manns' front door. This was to be his last visit before Christmas. University term had finished and the campus was deserted. He had only stayed in Armidale to be with Marny.

He found her resting in an armchair, daydreaming. "A penny for your thoughts."

Marny started, for she hadn't heard Peter come in, then she smiled. "Actually, I was thinking about you."

"Nice thoughts?" Peter sat down on her bed.

"Sort of....Are you leaving today?"

"Sorry–but yes. I've overstayed already. Dad's flat-out harvesting."

"You're awfully kind, Peter."

"Stop! Spare my blushes!"

"But you are. You've been helping me for so long and now you're leaving to help your dad."

"I enjoy it," Peter said. "Dad wants to work the combine harvester day and night while the weather holds. The men are there but he really needs *my* help as well. Generally he's been doing the night shift."

Marny smiled. "Shall I lend you Cas when the tractor breaks down?"

"Wouldn't he get tired harvesting two hundred hectares?"

"O.K., I won't then."

Peter got off the bed and sat on the arm of her chair. "Cas stays at Mr. Szechy's until Saturday. Mrs. Rowbotham is coming up on Sunday to collect you and to bring him back."

"I can't wait," said Marny. "I've been imagining riding again for these last five weeks."

"Don't be disappointed. I've tried with him but I'll never be as serious a rider as you."

"At least you rode him." Peter was too modest to tell Marny how much Cas had improved. But Tibor had telephoned her every week and described their progress. The big horse was accepting the bit now; his transitions and halts were becoming smoother; and his timing over jumps was increasingly accurate. Cas no longer made his big novice leaps. Now he cleared obstacles with only a few centimetres to spare.

"Did you like working with Tibor?" Marny asked.

"They weren't like any lessons I'd ever had before. He watches each stride the horse takes and notices every mistake I make. After thirty minutes I was exhausted."

"I know what you mean," agreed Marny.

"But on the other hand, it's not just a sport—riding with Tibor—it's an art."

"I suppose we can't keep saying how lucky we are...."

Peter was fumbling in his pocket and didn't answer. He brought out a very small packet, about the size of a match-box, and gave it to her.

"It was my mother's," he said. "Open it on Christmas day."

Then he kissed the top of her head and went away.

Marny was turning the box over and over and feeling lonely when Candida bubbled in, full of Christmas plans.

"I just saw Peter driving away. He looked awfully sad."

"I am too," said Marny. "He's gone back to help his dad. When are you off?"

"Tomorrow. It'll be our first Christmas apart for ten years, Marny." Then she asked anxiously, "Do you think they'll like me?" She was going to spend the holiday with Barry and his parents at Wagga Wagga.

"Of course they'll like you." Marny looked thoughtful. "You know, I can't believe its happening, Candy. We're nearly grown up."

"Speak for yourself. I'm quite grown up already." And she danced round the room holding Whisky up by his front legs while he growled ineffectually at her. "Still, I'm glad you stopped fighting off that boyfriend of yours.

"Candy, how could I have been so mean? How awful I was to him at Shooter's. Why didn't you stop me?"

"I thought I did in the end."

"You're an incorrigible mischief-maker." The two girls hugged each other. "Have a wonderful time."

"Have a good Christmas yourself."

"How can I when my best boyfriend and best girlfriend won't be there?"

Sunday finally arrived and Mrs. Rowbotham's yellow car drew up outside the Mann house with a hiss of airbrakes. Marny ran to greet her, although the effort made her appendix scar throb. Mrs. Rowbotham was terribly excited at the prospect of seeing Tibor.

"Meeting a real champion! Fancy! Shall I bow?"

Marny winced." Don't *please* do anything special, Mrs. Rowbotham. He's really quite shy."

"Oh good, that won't matter. I'm excellent at putting shy people at their ease."

Mrs. Rowbotham drove fast and absent-mindedly. Marny was glad to arrive at Glen Innes safely.

"Oh, it's you," said Tibor as he came out to greet them. He acted as if he had last seen Marny only last week, not six weeks ago.

Mrs. Rowbotham appeared to be precisely twice the girth of the lean riding master. She coloured and simpered as Tibor bent over her plump hand and kissed it gallantly. Marny left them and ran ahead, her heart beating with expectation as she slipped into the strawfilled garage with its warm, horsey smell. Casanova had been dozing, resting his off-hind, his eyes closed. When he heard her footsteps he woke up and nickered a welcome. Marny flung her arms round his neck.

"What's this?" boomed Mrs. Rowbotham, coming in to investigate. Cas jumped backwards, startled.

"It's only Mrs. Rowbotham," the girl whispered into his torn ear.

"I must tell you, Marny, that horse becomes *handsomer* every time I see him."

Tibor said crisply, "We will wait until you have built up strength again, Marianne. Then I shall test you both over the jumps."

"He's been going so well for Peter, I'm afraid he won't go so well for me."

"The secret of instructing," Tibor said quietly, "is to know how much to ask of a pupil."

Marny flushed and bit her lip. Will I never learn not to doubt him? she thought.

Tibor continued, "Your father has been pressing me again to allow you to enter competitions. Although it is early, the horse is keen, and so are you. I gave my permission for your debut at Europambla."

"The Novice One Day Event! Oh Mr. Szechy! I always wanted to enter but I never knew enough about dressage."

"Let us hope you do now."

"What *is* the One Day Event?" asked Mrs. Rowbotham.

"I will explain to you, Madame," said Tibor.

Marny was delighted that her two friends had taken a fancy to one another. Mrs. Rowbotham was so impressed with Tibor that occasionally she remembered to lower her voice.

"Eventing," Tibor explained, "derives from cavalry practice. A One Day Event comprises three parts, dressage, cross country, and show jumping. The cavalry horse had to obey his rider implicitly. Their lives or those of their comrades could depend on it—hence the dressage phase. Then the horse had to carry his rider at full gallop across country and jump any obstacle in the way. So we make the cross country phase."

"Like bringing the good news from Ghent to Aix?" asked Marny, remembering the old poem.

"Something like that. The horse must also prove his fitness and stamina so that after the cross country phase, he completes a show jumping course."

"All on one day?" Mrs. Rowbotham said. "That's quite an effort."

"Eventing will be Casanova's introduction to show jumping," Tibor told her.

"There's a Three Day Event at the Sydney Royal Show, if I remember rightly."

144

"That is correct, Mrs. Rowbotham. When Casanova qualifies during the Novice One Day Event at Europambla, he can enter for the Sydney Royal in March."

When Casanova qualifies?....Are you joking?" Marny looked incredulous.

"Do I generally joke about training, Marianne?"

"Sorry. I keep making stupid remarks today." Marny took both Tibor's hands in hers. Very seriously she promised, "I will work hard, and Casanova will too."

"That's the beauty of that horse. He always does," said Tibor.

"Wasn't that too too exciting for words!" cried Mrs. Rowbotham as she swerved the yellow car on to the road back to Armidale. Marny pitied poor Cas swaying about in the float behind and crossed her fingers for him. "You are a lucky girl," went on her companion.

"I know," Marny replied. "Sometimes it seems like a dream and I think I'll wake up and there'll be no more Casanova and no more Tibor Szechy."

"They both appear solid enough to me," said Mrs. Rowbotham.

Marny rode Casanova every day until Christmas. Each day she asked a little more from herself, and after about ten rides she was as supple and relaxed astride Casanova as ever she had been before the operation. She felt the dramatic improvement in his paces: he was like a machine that worked perfectly as long as she pressed the right buttons. However, an incorrect push sparked off a small explosion.

"Why can't I keep my left leg *on* you?" Marny moaned as Casanova's hindquarters drifted out to the left. With a determined effort she checked her position in the saddle and pushed him into a stronger trot, forcing him to straighten out and step on one track again. This time the horse flowed down the long side of the orchard between the apple and cherry trees.

"Great stuff!"

Marny twisted round in her saddle to see Mark Thomas leaning on the orchard gate.

"Thanks, but it's Mr. Szechy's work."

"Maybe I should send Pye up with you one weekend. He could learn a thing or two."

"You haven't been riding much this last year, have you?"

"Nope. Too many sick animals."

"Does Pye mind?"

"I don't think he does. He and Moonlight spend their time gossiping over the fence like a couple of old ladies."

"I'm glad they're company for each other." Then Marny told Mark about the plans for Casanova's first competition. The vet was pleased. "We'll all come and watch you at Europambla. But I came today to ask you a favour."

"What's up?"

"There's a pony with a hernia out on Long Swamp road. I need your help with the anaesthetic."

"Just give me five minutes," Marny called, pushing Casanova into an energetic trot.

"She's got guts. She deserves to win," thought Mark.

Chapter 21

It was always warm and sunny at Christmas. Trudy and Sigi remembered colder European Christmases but Marny had only known blue skies. Still, the Manns kept up some of their family traditions. For Christmas breakfast Trudy always made pancakes which she served with black cherry jam, and Sigi made coffee with scoops of double whipped cream.

"Merry Christmas, *Liebchen.*" Her parents hugged and kissed her as she came into breakfast from the stable yard carrying bundles of freshly picked flowers.

Sigi got up from the table. "I've got to be at the hospital, but I'll return before our guests arrive."

"Dad! Surely not on Christmas day?"

"You can't stop your father, Marny," Trudy said ruefully. "Medicine is his love as well as his work."

"When I'm qualified as a vet I won't go out on calls on holidays."

"Of course, you will too," said her mother. And they began happily to clear up the kitchen and prepare the house for the Christmas dinner.

The Thomas clan arrived by mid-morning. Micky and Paul were blowing tin whistles that Candida had mischievously put in their stockings, knowing that she would not be there to hear the racket. Whisky took one look at the proceedings and retired to the stables, joining Ugly Duckling who was stretched out smugly on a bag of oats. There was a great exchange of presents and greetings and kisses; no one heard Tibor Szechy's hesitant rap on the front door. Then Sigi saw him through the window and hurried outside to conduct the old man indoors. The two men embraced.

"We are happy you were able to come," said Sigi formally.

Tibor bowed and presented Marny with a large cardboard box decorated with silhouettes of horses cut out of black paper.

"How charming!" cried Trudy.

"Thank you. I used to love paper-cutting once." Tibor looked round at the family party. He seemed glad to be with them.

Shyly Marny presented him with a parcel, waiting until Tibor began to unwrap it before unwrapping her own.

"Thank you Marianne. What a truly thoughtful present." Tibor held up the big coloured photograph for everyone to look at. Peter had snapped Ugly Duckling and Casanova in the orchard, the cat perched on the chestnut's back, fast asleep, the horse looking with alert eyes straight into the camera.

"But Mr. Szechy!" Marny was most embarrassed at what Tibor had given her.

"It's not for you, my dear," he said "but for your horse." The bridle was handmade—a rolled leather snaffie, old but in perfect condition.

"It's lovely. I must go and try it on Casanova straight away.

Everyone followed her down to the stable. As the noisy procession approached, Whisky and Ugly Duckling looked at one another resignedly and walked with dignity out of the yard. The bridle fitted Cas as if made for him and showed off the beauty of his classic head.

The three older Thomas children were clambering all over the yard as they usually did, ignoring their mother's pleas for them to be "good quiet children."

"Story, story," they chanted, turning to their father.

"No, I don't feel like it," replied Andrew Thomas, attempting to shoo them away.

"But we're waiting, ever so good," cried Paul as he, Susy, and Louise strung themselves out on the paddock rail.

"I shall tell you a story," said Tibor Szechy in his slow voice. "But will you mind if it has an unhappy ending?"

"No, we won't," cried the children. "Begin, begin!"

"One Christmas, long ago, before any of you were born, it was snowing...."

"Snowing?" cried the children.

"Yes, it was snowing. We were in Hungary, far away from Australia."

"We know where Hungary is," called Louise.

"You'd better stop interrupting, or Mr. Szechy won't tell you the story," warned Andrew.

The children fell silent and Tibor continued. "As dusk fell, Lise and I stood at the window watching the falling snow.

"Who was Lise?" asked Paul.

"Lise was my wife. And we lived in a farmhouse with my parents. My mother had been baking for weeks, and the house was filled with the smell of poppy-seed rolls and Christmas cookies. My mother liked to do everything exactly the same way that *her* mother had.

"On this evening, the night before Christmas, we lit the candles on the Christmas tree and as the heat of the wax warmed the pine needles the whole room filled up with the familiar Christmassy smell." Tibor smiled at the gaily dressed children sitting on the rails in the bright sunshine.

"Now the farm children came in to receive their presents. They were all dressed in fur caps and boots and fur-lined gloves. Even so, their noses were red with cold." Paul rubbed his own nose. How funny! Imagine being cold on Christmas day! "The children played games and sang carols. We all loved the sound of their laughter because there were no children living in our house."

"Why not?" asked Louise.

"Because Lise and I never had any," said Tibor sadly.

"Shush," said Susy. "Let him get on with the story."

"Well, the party was going on gaily when the coachman stumbled in the door. His name was Jozsci and he'd been celebrating the festive season—with apricot brandy. He could hardly speak, but he stood there blinking his eyes in the bright lights and mumbling, 'At the stables. At the stables.' I followed him quickly, for I was afraid something was wrong with the horses. Ours was a horse farm: we bred horses.

"In the stables I could see nothing wrong. Jozsci followed me, swaying on his feet as he held up the lantern. The contented mares in their boxes looked at us with surprise as we passed by. In the last box lay a mare named Jacint and her two-day-old foal. He'd been born early and was weak. Jacint was lying very still. I held my breath, then....we heard a thin wail. Jacint's foal lay cuddled beside her, but tucked between her front legs was a white bundle. The white bundle was wailing.

"Jozsci mumbled, 'Thought I was dreaming, sir. It's been here a couple of hours, maybe, and the mare won't get up in case she steps on it. Never seen the likes of that.'

"Lise had followed me down to the stables. She bent down and picked up the bundle, and without a word she ran back to the house, the bundle wrapped in her shawl."

"What was it?"

"A baby, stupid," said Susy scathingly to her younger sister.

"But whose baby, Mr. Szechy?"

"We never found out. Someone put him in the stable, knowing we'd look after him. He was a little boy and we called him Pisti.

"But that night the baby cried without ceasing. We gave him bottles of milk and took turns carrying him, but still he wouldn't stop. By Christmas morning we were worn out. Jozsci came up with the answer. 'This brat wants to be in the stable, he likes the smell there. He wants Jacint. *That's* where he's meant to be.'

"We'd tried everything else and failed, so we took his advice. The moment Lise entered the stable with the wailing baby in her arms, the screams grew less and died away, and soon the child closed his eyes and fell asleep. Pisti stayed in the stable, we arranged a crib for him in Jacint's box, and Lise used to go there to give him his bottles."

"But where was his *real* Mummy?" asked Louise in a worried voice.

"She never came back. Pisti grew up with the horses. Later on, when he was a toddler, he would move between their legs. None of the horses would ever kick him. Pisti was on Jacint's back long before he could walk, and he could ride properly at the age of five, clearing little jumps, with one hand on Jacint's long mane and the other waving in the air. Mind you, all this without a saddle."

"I bet he didn't like school," said Paul, who hated it himself.

"You are quite right. He didn't do well at school. He also preferred the company of animals to other children, and he set up an animal hospital in the barn. He kept injured birds, broken-legged frogs, a blind puppy, or mice he rescued from the stable cats."

"I expect he grew up to be a vet like Uncle Mark."

"I told you it was a sad story," said Tibor. "Let me finish. When Pisti was six he was given his own saddle and he was a fine rider. He had a lovely way with animals. Sometimes you remind me of him, Marny. His happiest times were on the back of a horse.

"Pisti was ten when war broke out. At first we carried on at the farm. I was training a Lipizzaner horse named Kaspar, and every day Pisti watched, sitting on the fence rail as you children are doing now. When he was twelve I allowed him to ride Kaspar. That's the best memory I have of him—almost the last."

"But where's Pisti now?"

"I'm coming to that. I was conscripted in 1942 and left the farm. Many, many things happened. Pisti and Kaspar vanished...."

"How could they vanish?" The children were astonished. Louise was biting her lip, trying not to cry.

"I don't really know," Tibor replied thoughtfully. "So many bad and terrible things happened in the war. Lise was killed by the invaders, but I heard that Pisti and Kaspar escaped together. Many people told of a boy riding a Lipizzaner without saddle or bridle, nothing but a piece of rope around his neck. Perhaps he too was shot down." Tibor sighed.

At this point Trudy came up and, slipping her arm through Tibor's, invited them all indoors to eat. The temporary sadness caused by Tibor's tale evaporated as they smelt Christmas dinner. This year Trudy had surpassed herself, and everyone ate until not another mouthful would go down.

After dinner Janey picked the sleeping Micky up out of the mess of Christmas wrappings on the carpet and took him down the hall to bed in Marny's room. The rest of them crowded into the sitting-room to talk and play games and sing carols until tea time.

When all the visitors had gone home and she was alone in her bedroom Marny unwrapped Peter's present. The tiny box contained an antique garnet pendant.

Chapter 22

The yellowing grass smelt of high summer as Marny walked down to the stable, still buttoning up her old overalls. Casanova poked his head over the door in surprise, not expecting her for another hour. The dew was sparkling in the early sunshine.

"Keep your head *down,*" she begged him, emptying his oats into the manger, "while I try to plait your mane." She stood on an upturned stable bucket, her pocket full of rubber bands, and began. She combed the already washed mane free of tangles, then damped the hair and divided it into eight equal hanks. The plaits were laid on the offside—for some obscure reason considered correct by the horse fraternity. "Damn. Why won't they lie evenly?" Marny grumbled, as the sixth plait worked loose. She untied and replaited it, wound a rubber band around the fluffy base, and tucked the free end back under the mane. When the eight plaits were completed, she stitched each one in place with black cotton. "You *do* look smart, even if I say so myself." Cas finished his oats and raised his head, his nose still sticky with remains of breakfast, just in time for Marny to plait his short golden forelock.

Next came his feet. Marny made a mixture of neatsfoot oil, mutton fat, and Stockholm tar, and rubbed it over the hooves and into the coronet. "Remember your flaky feet when I first brought you home, boy?" Casanova looked at her solemnly. Of course he did. When she had finished she brought out a tin of Blackett and worked the awful-looking paste into the hooves. As the paste dried, the hoof was coloured a shiny pitch black. Marny shook her watch and grimaced. "Goodness, it's getting late. All your fancy dress takes ages." She started rubbing the soft body-brush over Casanova's already shiny clean coat. He had been shampooed yesterday afternoon."

"At least *you* don't roll," she told him, recalling sadly how Sure Smile used to ruin her shampoos. She brushed the chestnut for nearly an hour, until the reflection of her own face appeared in his gleaming hide. Then she borrowed Candida's trick and finished off the grooming by polishing with a piece of silk. The fully-risen sun filtered stray beams into the stable and striped golden bars on the chestnut's coat. Putting a light blue dustsheet over her handiwork to keep off the dust, Marny patted Cas and ran up to breakfast.

"I can't possibly, Mum," she cried, regarding with horror the plate of chops and eggs Trudy thought a sustaining enough meal before a competition.

"What's all this nonsense?" Sigi was up early too. The excitement affected the whole household—except for Ugly Duckling.

"Sorry, Dad." Marny smiled nervously and began toying with the food.

Sigi looked disapproving. "I don't want any of this prima donna behaviour."

Marny rebelled. "Don't you ever get nervous before something important?"

"I never stop eating."

"You haven't answered the question, Dad."

Trudy tactfully took away Marny's plate of half-finished food. "Run and get ready. They'll be here to fetch you in half an hour."

Marny dressed quickly, humming cheerfully. "I'm glad I don't have to justify myself to Mum and Dad any more," she thought. "They're backing me up all the way." Peter's pendant hung on its thin gold chain under her blouse: she touched it now for luck.

At the sound of a horn she rushed outside to find that the big yellow car had arrived, towing the float. She sighed with relief when Peter's head came out of the driving window and he waved.

"Hullo, Marny. All set?"

Mrs. Rowbotham said, "My, Marny, you're looking pretty as a picture—isn't she, Peter? Are you two getting spliced one day?"

"Let's think about that after the show, Mrs. Rowbotham, shall we?"

Casanova walked quietly up the now-familiar ramp, followed by Ugly Duckling, tail erect. The cat had enjoyed a good doze in the stable and was ready for adventure. "No you don't, puss. No eventing for cats today," said Peter, scooping the indignant animal out of the float.

"Oh, Peter! Uggs won't speak to you for months now," cried Marny.

"That's too bad. I can't look after you, Cas, Mrs. Rowbotham, *and* Ugly Duckling."

After a ninety-minute run they reached the stone boundary wall that marked the Europambla property. Beside the gate was a wooden signboard on which someone had tacked a red arrow pointing left. Following the directions, they drove down a rutty track leading to the cattle-yard where the One Day Event was to take place. The dressage arena was a sanded oblong, bordered with a white fence. Behind it, inside the oval racetrack, was the show-jumping course, gay with flags and coloured jumps. There were forty-two horses and riders competing. Peter and Mrs. Rowbotham went over to the display board to find Marny's draw for the dressage.

"Good!" Peter saw that Marny wouldn't be riding until eleven o'clock. "Cas'll have time to get settled."

Marny saddled up and began to exercise Cas quietly, keeping half an eye on the other competitors performing in the ring. "They look frightfully good, boy." Marny was acquainted with some of the riders, but many more of them seemed to know her. The story in the newspaper had made Cas well known in the district.

The Shooter float was parked under a clump of wattles. Alex had brought two horses: Mirabelle and a new hunter called Too True. Marny supposed that Alice would be riding Mirabelle, and she recognised Sue Blunt, a friendly buck-toothed girl who sometimes rode for Alex. Since the battle with Cas he hadn't been riding himself. When Alex saw her, he called her over.

"Got him out today, have you? Bit soon, isn't it?" He smiled at her in a friendly way, but Marny shivered.

"The test of preparedness will come in a few minutes," said a familiar voice beside her.

"Oh, Mr. Szechy, you've made it! How wonderful! Alex, this is my riding master. Tibor Szechy....Alex Shooter." Alex looked rather discomfited. He nodded curtly and turned back to his horses.

"All right, Marianne?" Tibor's smile was kind. "Remember— *Your line and your speed;* and *Go forward, go straight.*"

"I will." And Marny set off calmly for the dressage arena.

The bell rang, and she was on her own. For the first few seconds she was conscious of her group of friends, watching and hoping. Then she forgot everything and began to concentrate. She remembered that Tibor had advised her to smile at the judges, and managed a shaky grin before tracking to the right at a working trot. Casanova performed the basic movements very well. His paces were smooth and balanced, his body supple, and his carriage gay and relaxed. The spectators clapped appreciatively as the test ended and Marny rode out of the arena on a loose rein.

"Good!" said Tibor, caressing Casanova as Marny reined in. "He did well. He was as nervous as you were."

"Was he?"

"Yes. He performed for you on a trust. All this was new to him."

"How selfish of me," murmured Marny. "I was only thinking of my own worries."

The scoreboard told the story of phase one. Casanova and Marianne Mann were points ahead of their nearest rivals. Marny scanned the board anxiously—she hadn't thought they had done as well as that. She caught a few whispers behind her: "That's the wild horse. "Got some foreign bloke training her." "Beautiful movement." "Stupid judging."

The loudspeaker boomed, "All competitors in phase two, show jumping, must jump in order of their dressage draw." Marny just had time for a quick snack with her family before she had to go to the start. She was trembling with excitement. Cas now

156

had a reputation to keep up. She rode up to the start beside the racecourse, thinking of the competition, her reins loose. Tibor walked beside her.

Then Cas saw the metal starting stalls. He stopped, stared, and snorted. A thousand memories chased across his mind. Who knows how horses remember? They do remember. They love and they hate. And Cas had hated racing. He squealed and reared, then careered forward in a series of wild bucks. The bystanders shouted and scattered in front of him. A woman's scream unnerved the horse further. Tibor had been left behind in the first plunge but now he limped forward and seized the bridle. Marny had lost her balance. Casanova gradually began to calm down as Tibor murmured to him. When the taut muscles relaxed, Tibor released his hold on the bridle. "Memories," he said. "He has too many. Go on now, and good luck."

There was no time to settle Casanova further before the bell rang and Marny had to go through the starting flags. She tried desperately to gain the gelding's attention, but Cas would not heed her. He blundered through the first jump, a low bush fence he could have trotted over, and lumbered towards the second, out of balance and careless. He knocked it down.

Then Marny made a decision. She pulled Cas up and turned away from the jumps and began to walk him in a circle on a loose rein. All the time she spoke gently to him, coaxing and soothing, trying to regain his attention. The crowd was silent. This had never happened before at Europambla. After all, there were rules to cope with. Every circle Marny and Casanova walked constituted an about-turn away from the next obstacle and so constituted a refusal fault. After the third circle, they would be eliminated. And every second over the time allotted meant another five penalty points. The stopwatch ticked inexorably. Half way round the second circle Marny felt Casanova relax. His ears pricked forward, then flicked back so that he could hear what she was saying to him. "Now, boy, steady. *Let's go!*"

There was a surge of power as Casanova lengthened stride for take-off. He thrust into the air, his legs tucked beneath him, his spine curved in a classic parabola over the jump. The course flashed by, horse and rider working as one. Neither of them heard the enthusiastic applause. Then Marny gently eased Casanova back to a trot as they passed the red finish flags.

"You were wonderful," she whispered into his torn ear.

Her family and friends had mixed feelings.

"Tough luck, Marny, you rode fabulously," Candida said encouragingly.

"You did end up well," said Trudy.

"Yes, but will he ever be reliable?" asked Sigi, clearly trying to hide his disappointment.

"Dad, be patient with him, and with me too," Marny pleaded. Sigi's rather annoyed expression softened as he saw how happy his daughter looked.

"I *would* have liked to show the Shooters up," said Janey Thomas.

"Never mind. Alex Shooter knows enough to judge Casanova's performance," said Mark.

Tibor Szechy was still silent. Marny glanced at him. His brown eyes were twinkling under his thick eyebrows. It wasn't the winning that mattered to Tibor, but the performance. Alice rode past them jauntily. Mirabelle had completed a clear round.

After what seemed an incredibly short time, Marny's number was called over the loudspeaker for the final phase, the cross country.

"Good luck!" said Peter.

"Be careful, *Leibchen.* God bless you," Trudy called.

"Take him quietly and enjoy yourselves," counselled Tibor.

"Ten seconds to go," cried the man with the stopwatch. "Five....four....three....two....one....go...."

Casanova shot forward across the flat valley towards the rolling hills, effortlessly clearing all obstacles put in his way. His long stride cut everything down to size. Not one other horse following the three-kilometre course could equal him.

Marny found herself smiling as they approached the last fence. Casanova was running like a two-year-old colt. He was happy. He steeplechased the last fence and galloped up the final slopes. When they halted at the finish, Cas was breathing deeply and regularly, as fit as he had been when he started. He could run another three kilometres easily.

"He's in A-1 condition," said Mark, after listening critically to the heartbeats.

Mrs. Rowbotham, oblivious to Mark's veterinary frown, was joyfully feeding Cas lumps of white sugar.

"Thank you," Marny said to the master. "We've done it."

"It is time I thanked you, Marianne," said the old man.

At the prize-giving Marny enthusiastically clapped the winners. Alice Shooter had won a rosette, having gained fourth place on Mirabelle. It was a creditable performance for the little mare.

"I've got the distinction of coming last with the most penalty faults," Marny laughed, not at all upset, happy they had finished the course. Even more important—Casanova hadn't been eliminated, and so he qualified for the Royal Show at Sydney.

"We're on our way, love," said Peter.

They drove away from Europambla in the dusk. Tomorrow the arena would be a cattle-yard again and the jumps would be dismantled. The drama was concluded for another twelve months.

Chapter 23

The 586-kilometre journey from Armidale to Sydney seemed to Peter and Marny to pass in a flash. With the utility pulling the float, they descended the mountain range of the New England tablelands, then went down about 900 metres into the coastal plains. These two steep altitude drops were called Moonbi One and Moonbi Two. The bitumen road skirted the mountains in a series of frightening twists and curves, so Peter drove very carefully in first gear. Casanova's head could be glimpsed through the perspex window in front of the float.

"He's never been so far with us before. I hope he's not worried."

"He's not. Uggs will reassure him if he's nervous."

"Did you pack the tins of cat food?"

"Don't start fussing, woman. Of course I did." They smiled at each other.

Marny reflected, "I wonder if I'd have come this far without Peter."

Reading her thoughts, Peter said. "You'd still be on the way to Sydney. Tibor would have seen to that."

"Maybe."

After they had successfully negotiated the mountains, they travelled across undulating plains planted with lush crops and fertile valleys stocked with fat cattle. Peter's farmer's eye noted with pleasure the agricultural prosperity around them. They decided to stop for lunch at Scone, famous for its racehorse studs. Casanova was unloaded in a small park just outside the town, in sight of a magnificent paddock where brood mares grazed, their foals at foot.

Ugly Duckling emerged from the float and rubbed himself against Marny's legs.

"O.K.," she said, "I can take a hint." Ugly Duckling pretended to hunt his cat food, scooping pieces out of the tin with his forepaw, tossing them in the air, and catching them before he settled down to the serious business of eating.

"Sorry, boy, just lucerne chaff and bran for you," Peter told Casanova as the horse rooted energetically in his feed bin, looking for cool, fresh oats.

"Strict instructions, Cas," Marny said firmly. *No work, no oats!* Mark was absolutely definite over it. Peter, what is 'Monday morning sickness'?"

"I know what Mark meant. I read about it in last term's course work. Only its proper name is azoturia."

"Azo—what?"

"—turia."

"Oh! But there must be a reason for the common name."

"There is. It comes from the old coaching days, when there were thousands of Australian Walers between the shafts. They travelled enormous distances and were well fed with barley and oats and corn. They rested on Sunday and were fed the same amount of food. Then on Mondays they were harnessed up and sent down the roads. Sometimes, after about fifteen kilometres, a horse would collapse between the shafts with the dreaded Monday morning sickness."

"How awful! But how could a good meal and a rest make a horse ill?"

"It sounds funny, doesn't it? It works like this: the grain supplies the horse with carbohydrates which he uses for energy while he's working. When he's resting he doesn't use them up in the same way, and the incompletely-broken-down carbohydrates, together with an intermediary product of digestion called tactic acid, accumulate in his muscles. He can't digest them or excrete them. Then, when he starts to work again, the tactic acid starts to eat into the muscle fibres, and he gets the acute symptoms of azoturia: collapse, muscle spasm, intense pain. He may also pass red-coloured urine, due to the breakdown of muscle tissue. For that reason the condition is sometimes known as blackwater. It can be fatal."

"What a horrible thing," said Marny with a grimace. Then she smiled. "But we're lucky. We know the dangers, and Cas won't ever get it." She watched the mares grazing. "D'you think Cas was born here?"

"Maybe. Some of our best Thoroughbreds are. Perhaps he's an accidental mating; a famous stallion sneaked into someone's farm and Cas was the result." Cas raised his head from his feed bucket and looked at them. "Accident, indeed!" he seemed to say. "My birth was more carefully planned than either of yours." His upper lip curled before he lowered his head to polish off the remains of his frugal lunch.

The rest of the journey was uneventful—just as well, for Marny had begun to worry. Was she too young to compete in the Three Day Event? Had she prepared enough? Was Cas ready? Then she thought about Tibor Szechy and she knew that he would never have agreed to let her enter if her fears were justifiable. "Relax," he would say to her now. "A good rider is never tense."

Peter drove into the city of Sydney in the early evening. The Blue Mountains hung purple in the distance and the traffic had begun to snarl up as they drove along one of the main arterial roads leading to the city centre and the showground. Marny sensed that Cas was worried by the constant braking as thoughtless drivers cut in front of the slow-moving float. "Thank goodness he's thoroughly bandaged," she thought.

The first thing that struck her, once they arrived at the showground, was the large number of expensive cars pulling luxurious horse floats. Their dented utility and painted wooden float looked out of place in the middle of all that affluence.

"Where there are horses there's always money," she remarked.

"It was the same in England," commented Peter.

"I suppose it would be. I've never really come across it before. It makes me wonder how I got here."

"Because you worked for it. You didn't have a groom to strap your horse and muck out the stable."

"No, but I bet we had a better trainer than lots of these wealthy riders."

The congestion was amazing: cars, trucks, floats, horses, and ponies, all milling around the too few officials. Everyone wanted keys for stables and feed rooms and permits for their cars. A thousand questions were being asked and none of them answered. Finally a tired and harassed Peter received their stable key and number. Gratefully, they unloaded Casanova and led him around to Block E where a box had been allocated. It was midnight before they managed to unpack all their gear. Peter looked dubiously into the loft above Casanova's stable where he had installed Marny's camping gear.

"Are you sure you'll be all right here?"

"Of course. I really do want to stay with Cas all the time. Lots of owners do. Besides, your dad's friends are expecting you— you must go."

"All right then. Sleep well. I'll be here in time to take you to breakfast."

Preparations for the start of the show went on all the next day. The atmosphere was excited and expectant. Overalled men rushed about everywhere. Huge colourful agricultural displays were taking shape, enormous piles of apples, cherries, bananas, pumpkins, tomatoes, and potatoes. Every centimetre of the eight-hectare site would be in use by the time the show opened. There were special pavilions to house machinery, cars, livestock, and floral exhibits. And there were the best, most beautiful horses Australia has to offer. Although they didn't meet anyone they knew, Peter and Marny wandered over the ground arm-in-arm, enjoying the sights and finding everyone friendly. When they had seen all they wanted, they returned to the stables. Peter began to groom Cas, rubbing over his chestnut coat until it glowed like brandy in a crystal glass.

"When does Mr. Szechy arrive?" asked Marny.

"He's flying down with your parents on the morning plane," said Peter, who had received all the messages from the friends with whom he was staying. "My dad will fly down too, and Mark is driving in with Mrs. Rowbotham. I'm going to give a stable party for you after the cross country. Everyone'll be here except for Barry and Candy."

Marny looked scared at the idea, but Peter hastened to reassure her. "It'll be great, Marny. The worst will be over by then, and we can relax. There'll only be the show jumping to go. Besides, your friends have come to see you. We ought to do something for them."

"I suppose you're right," said Marny hesitantly. "It might be fun."

"Now you've got an hour's roadwork with Casanova and then your schooling on the flat."

"I don't know which of us is fitter, Cas or me."

"You've lost weight."

"I know. The more I lose, the more lead I have to carry in the saddle bags. But we're used to it."

Soon after Peter had finished grooming, the familiar figures of Alice and Alex Shooter appeared walking down the aisle of the stables.

"How did *you* get such a good position?" asked Alex.

"We're stuck up on the far hill."

"Just luck," Peter replied.

Alice ignored Peter. She had been particularly disagreeable to him since the night of Blair's party. She secretly wished that he were *her* boyfriend, and was piqued by his interest in Marny Mann.

"Is that horse ready for a 3 D.E.?" She squinted critically at Casanova.

"Watch out!" cried Marny. Cas had recognised Alex, his old enemy, and suddenly he snapped at him, catching the man's sleeve in his teeth. Alex wrenched his arm away. There was a large rip in his smart jacket.

"Still incurably vicious, I see," Alex snarled, his affability vanishing.

"Dear me," said Alice, nastily. "You'd better be careful, Marny. You don't want any complaints *here* do you?"

Marny felt her temper rising. Why do they always try to ruin everything? she thought. But Peter mollified the Shooters by apologising politely and inviting them to Marny's stable party.

165

Alex's scowl lifted as he recollected that Charles Cooke-Finch would be present, and that he would probably bring along influential friends.

"Alrighty. I'm a long-suffering bloke. We'll come to see you later."

Marny was still shaking with nerves and exasperation.

"Don't reduce yourself to their level," Peter warned her. *"They* can't help themselves. He legged her up on to Casanova. "Come on, let's go." He led her out of the stable complex towards a big park set aside for exercising the horses.

The day for the dressage phase dawned. Marny was so nervous she could barely dress. She hadn't eaten any breakfast earlier and now she was regretting it. "Dad's right," she thought. "A full tummy does give you something to go on." Her stomach seemed to be curling up involuntarily to hit her diaphragm, then dropping with a thump, sending waves of nausea through her body.

"Where are you?" It was Trudy's voice, a welcome, familiar sound. Marny poked her head out of the loft and saw her mother below, carrying a large meat pie and a bottle of chocolate milk. "Not home cooking, but solid and wholesome. I know you won't have eaten."

"Great, Mrs. Mann." Peter emerged from the stable. "I couldn't get her to swallow a thing."

"I've some for you, too," Trudy said. "Mark is bringing it."

Soon the whole Armidale contingent was gathered at the stable, drinking and chatting, and in this friendly atmosphere Marny felt some of her tension vanish. Then Tibor Szechy arrived. He was limping badly, for walking over the showground tired him. He hadn't enough strength to clear the ground at each stride.

"How has Casanova settled, Marny?" he asked.

"Better than I have, Mr. Szechy. I'm scared."

"You must relax. If you don't, I'll have you doing some exercises."

"O.K., O.K. I'm relaxed," Marny laughed. Peter led the old man into the tack room to inspect the cleaned gear.

"Bring me a sponge," said Tibor. "I want to put the finishing touches to that saddle."

"But we've done everything," Peter said reproachfully.

"You have been most diligent," replied Tibor. But after a few minutes' work he had brought a new and brilliant shine to the leather.

By the time Marny was dressed, her state of shock had returned. She couldn't speak properly, and just nodded when anyone spoke to her. Peter and Tibor knew exactly how she was feeling and left her alone; but Mrs. Rowbotham kept trying to cheer her up. So Sigi said, "Let's go to the dressage arena early, Mrs. Rowbotham. Then we can reserve our seats."

"Jolly good show." They set off together, and Marny gulped with relief.

"That should do it," said Trudy as she patted an escaping hair from Casanova's plaited mane back into place. She sprayed his plaits with hair spray, then stepped back, satisfied, to look at the magnificent sight of the chestnut prepared for the show ring.

As Marny rode down towards the playing fields where the tests were being held she heard one spectator saying to another, "My word, I haven't seen a horse like that for twenty years."

"Yes. The typical old English Thoroughbred."

You wouldn't have said that if you'd seen Cas last year, thought Marny, delighted.

At a quarter past twelve they were ready to enter the dressage arena for their debut into one of the hardest, toughest, and most glamorous competitions the Royal Show has to offer. The gruelling tests over the next three days would successfully sort out the thirty-odd competitors. Many of them would not finish.

"I do feel sick. I must look awful." Marny felt her stomach churn. But she didn't look sick; in fact, the spectators thought her to be one of the more polished and better presented competitors. When the bell rang, she heard calls of "Good luck!" and "We're with you!" from her family and friends. In a moment she recovered. Her stomach settled, and she patted Casanova's neck. "Do your best," she whispered. "We're on."

Casanova flicked both his ears backwards to listen. Then he moved forward into an active working trot, first in a circle outside the arena and then straight down the white-chalked centre line to come to a square halt at the "X". Marny saluted the judges, following Tibor's advice, and smiled at them. The test began to flow easily, from the result of months of painstaking application. Cas moved even better than he had done at Europambla, only three months before. His tracking was absolutely true, front and back. He moved on Marny's line and at the speed she dictated, and yet his own spirited personality was expressed in every movement. Marny sat completely still, her aids invisible. The big horse appeared to float in extension above the ground. The spectators were spellbound.

Marny heard the noise before Casanova did. She broke concentration and looked around. Bearing down on them from the outer edge of the playing fields were several Rugby League players out on a fitness run in the park. They were dressed in vivid green-and-white striped socks and jerseys, and the thudding of their boots shattered the orderly calm of the dressage arena. Shocked officials rushed out to head them off, but too late.

"Quiet! Get *out* of here! This is a Royal Show Equestrian competition!"

Casanova took genuine fright, letting out one of his high-pitched squeals. He reared, then spun around to face the intruders, snorting and stamping, his legs slightly splayed, nostrils flared. The men had meant no harm, and as quickly as they had arrived they departed. Casanova watched until they were out of sight before he could be persuaded to continue.

The second half of the test lacked the brilliance of the first. The horse's concentration had been broken, and the damp sweat patch on his neck showed what a fright he had received. Nevertheless, his movements were fluid, accurate and correct. As Marny rode out of the arena, everyone clapped as hard as they could.

"Brilliant test." "Hard luck." "What a mover!" "Can't be helped."

At the end of the day the scoreboard showed that Casanova was lying tenth in a field of thirty-four.

"You did your best," Marny told Cas as she settled him down for an early night. "It wasn't your fault if a crowd of footballers chose to come and disturb you."

Ten....nine....eight....seven....six....five....four....three....two....one....go! Marny and Casanova whipped forward and galloped down the grassy track towards the first steeplechase jump. The cross country phase of the Three Day Event comprised four sections covering twenty-four kilometres. First came six-and-a half kilometres of roads and tracks to be ridden at a moderate pace, with no bonus points awarded for speed. Casanova came in from this barely warmed up. He was fit and ready to commence section two, the steeplechase, three kilometres and fifteen fences set down the Randwick Racecourse, testing speed and jumping ability. Bonus points were awarded on this test, and every competitor tried to pick up as many as possible. After the steeplechase there was a further six-and-a-half kilometres of roads and tracks before the climax....eight kilometres of rugged cross country, including twenty-four jumps—the most gruelling test of all.

Casanova swept through the steeplechase course like the wind. After the first 120-centimetre brush fence had been cleared he picked up speed, his breathing deep and regular. Marny had never galloped so fast. She now knew for certain that her horse, her Casanova, must have been a racehorse. At the two-kilometre turn she looked out for the Armidale contingent, clustered in a tight group close to the fence. Tibor and Peter both had stop-watches. As she flew past, Tibor raised his arm and turned his thumb down—the prearranged signal. If Marny had needed to speed up to win maximum bonus points Tibor was to give a "thumbs up." They had barely considered the possibility that Casanova would gallop too *fast*.

"Steady, boy," Marny whispered. "Steady." Casanova flicked his ears back to hear the quiet voice. Without realising it, he slipped back into three-quarter pace, cleared the last fence in one stride, and galloped down towards the winning post and the photo-finish cameras.

Tibor and Peter were waiting for her.

"I couldn't have believed it," Marny gasped as she slid out of the saddle.

"I know," replied her riding master. "I realised what he was the first day you brought him to me."

170

Fifteen minutes later Marny was remounted and off on the second and final run of roads and tracks. During the gentle trots and easy canters through the park adjacent to the showground, Casanova recovered his wind completely. Mark Thomas had often commented on Casanova's "ventilation capacity." Marny was still panting, breathing shallowly, but Casanova was back to normal.

Ten....nine....eight....seven....six....five....four....three....two....one....go! Casanova shot forward once again into the final phase—the cross country. The going was heavy in some places, and the horses had to drag themselves through deep sand. The jumps blended into the hilly sandy country, merging naturally with the native vegetation. Four of them were especially difficult. One was a huge box of railway sleepers set half-way down a steep slope. But Marny need not have worried. As they jumped it, she had the incredible sensation of flying out into space. Casanova floated through the air, dropping to earth a considerable distance down the slope.

The next problem was a water jump in the dam. Marny had stripped down the day before and waded into the water to test its depth. She found that beyond the jump the floor dropped so sharply that a horse would have to swim, but if the rider made a sharp left turn on landing he would have to cope only with shallow water. Cas approached the dam too fast. Marny asked him to check, but by this time he was not attending—the thrill of the gallop in his blood. There was only one thing to do. She straightened up into dressage position, dropped her weight into the deepest part of the saddle, and pushed Casanova *hard* with her legs, forcing him into a half halt. It worked. The chestnut shortened his long stride just in time. Over the fence—into the water—a sharp left turn—and safely out on the far side of the dam.

The third difficult obstacle was number eleven—a large concrete drain nearly two metres wide, full of fast-flowing water. A single rail was placed across the centre about a metre above it. Casanova was apprehensive. The sound of the water gurgling and splashing loudly against the concrete sides of the drain unsettled him. But as he tried to shorten stride in order to refuse, Marny began to ride him forward, using hand, heels, and voice.

She rode as she had never ridden before. Tibor was watching them through binoculars, willing her not to make any mistakes.

Casanova had to respond to such forceful riding. The drain was cleared with quite a distance to spare, and he still had enough energy to kick up behind and squeal his indignation at such rough treatment.

"Good boy!" Marny gasped. "We've nearly made it."

The second–last jump was a nasty apex, or in-and-out, depending on how you wished to ride it. When Marny had walked the course with Tibor they had decided to angle the jump so that Cas could take one long stride and then jump out the other side. Now, with most of the jumps safely negotiated, he was still galloping well within himself. So she took a chance and, remembering Tibor's words: "When in doubt, ride forward," she set Cas boldly at the dead centre of the apex. With a mighty leap the big horse spanned it and thundered on to the last jump, an easy post-and-rails. The final 400 metres was flat, and there was a chance of picking up bonus points if Cas had enough strength left for a sprint.

"Can you do it, boy?" Marny whispered, leaning low over his steaming neck. In answer Casanova summoned up that extra bit of courage and stamina that was in his heritage. Labouring for breath, nearly spent after travelling some twenty-four kilometres, he surged forward once again. His powerful quarters thrust under his body, propelling him forward at tremendous speed. Marny felt the stinging wind whistle past her and heard the cheers of the crowd. Cas heard them too and, champion that he was, flattened out to charge through the flags as if he were finishing a 1600-metre race.

As Marny eased Casanova back to a walk, the cheers subsided. Friends, acquaintances, even people she hadn't met before lent a hand to unsaddle Cas, cool him down, and check that Marny weighed in correctly before she was allowed to relax. Soon Casanova was back in the stable, resting on a thick bed of straw and munching oats, absently swishing his tail at flies. No one looking at him now could have guessed that only an hour ago he had galloped twenty-four kilometres as if his heart would burst. Marny was also resting on her canvas stretcher in the loft, looking down at the horse and Ugly Duckling, and feeling quiet and content.

Just as she was drifting off into pleasant daydreams, Peter came rushing in, full of excitement. Casanova had won maximum bonus points in the steeplechase and the cross country. He had battled his way from tenth place, after the dressage, to third.

Others had been less successful. Eight horses had been eliminated in the cross country, and one poor animal had lost its life at the water jump. Alex Shooter's Mirabelle had been another casualty. Apparently Alex had tried to make up for previous neglect and had over-fed the mare, ignoring the dictum "feed grain according to work done." Mirabelle had collapsed at the second fence, and the vet in attendance had diagnosed azoturia.

Chapter 24

"I didn't realise you'd asked so many people," Marny whispered to Peter as the guests began arriving at Stable 605, Block E.

"I didn't," he said, grinning back at her. "People just want to meet you. You're famous now."

The feed room filled up rapidly with a chattering crowd, and huge supplies of beer and soft drinks appeared. Marny guessed that Charles Cooke-Finch must have organised the party.

"I knew Casanova when he was a skinny, savage fireball." Mrs. Rowbotham, an imposing sight in an orange jumpsuit, could be heard holding forth to a group of admirers.

"Why isn't my horse finishing his feeds?" A pretty blonde was trying to get free advice from Mark Thomas. "Maybe you're feeding him too much," the vet replied, brusquely. Discomfited, the girl retired and began to ask someone else the name of the best saddler in Sydney.

Sigi sat on a bale of straw, balancing a glass of beer and a plate of potato chips, and looking uncomfortable. Luckily a fellow doctor, John Bridges, came up and introduced himself.

The doctor had taken up riding ten years ago, at the age of forty-five. "I got tired of following my wife and daughters around the horse shows," he said, chuckling, so I bought an old cob and started to learn myself."

"Don't you dare do that at your age," said Trudy, looking fiercely at her husband.

"Not I, not I", Sigi reassured her. "How long was it before you felt competent on a horse, John?"

"A few months. But my patients called me 'Autumn Leaves' for a while, I was on the ground so much."

"Mm," said Sigi thoughtfully.

Alice Shooter made a dramatic late entrance with her father. Marny was surprised to see her. Didn't she want to stay with her sick mare? Apart from Mrs. Rowbotham, Alice was the most eye-catching female in the room. Her sweater was as low as it could be without failing off, and the contrast between her red hair and purple jeans was electrifying.

"*Wow!* Who brought *her?*" exclaimed one of the handsome young 3 D.E. riders.

"Does she ride as well?" asked another, a fair-haired lad.

"She competed today on Mirabelle," Peter told them.

"I remember. The mare collapsed. My, she's got a temper," recalled the fair-haired boy, gently removing himself from Alice's vicinity.

Alex shook Marny's hand." Your horse did well. I'll be the first to admit it."

"We had rotten luck with Mirabelle. But she'll soon be fit again, and then we'll give you a run for your money," Alice said, glowering.

"Alice, hold your tongue." Alex was exasperated. He didn't like losing any more than his daughter did, but he was better at concealing his poor sportsmanship. He made a renewed effort to be friendly. "Did you know Bob Kinsey was out of hospital, Marny?"

"I am glad. So there's no one against Cas any more."

"Not after today's performance. You know, Marny, you could come and train him at my place. We've got better jumps...."

Marny was dumbfounded. How could Alex possibly believe that she would ever let Cas near the Shooter academy again? But she didn't want to seem rude, so she ignored what he had said and turned to Alice. "Let me introduce you to Grant Davies. He shared the feed room with me."

Alice's discontented expression rapidly altered as the good-looking young maxi shook hands with her, his eyes riveted to her exposed bosom.

178

The party was in full swing when three strangers appeared. All of them were well dressed in dark suits, and one of them carried a polished cane. They scanned the crowd as if looking for someone, and then one of them spotted Tibor.

"Mr. Szechy?" he asked.

"Yes, that is my name," replied Tibor. "But I have not had the pleasure of meeting you gentlemen...."

"Let me remedy that," said the man. "I am Anthony Banks, President of the Equestrian Association of Australia. These are my colleagues Horatio Anderson and Howard Keen-Smith, both on the Executive Council."

Horatio Anderson beamed broadly. "It is an *honour* and a wonderful *surprise* to have you with us in the flesh, Mr. Szechy." He seized Tibor by the hand and shook it vigorously. "I saw you jump at Munich in 'thirty-six," he added with pride.

"We are hoping, Mr. Szechy, to persuade you to give some of our Olympic candidates the benefit of your valuable experience," said Anthony Banks.

"But how did you know who *I* was?" asked Tibor.

"Pure chance," replied Howard Keen-Smith. "We were discussing the performance of that big chestnut in the dressage yesterday, and someone commented that he'd clearly been trained by an expert. Well, what did you expect? I thought I knew every dressage expert in Australia. I became curious. I made enquiries. And here we are.

Anthony Banks turned to the wide-eyed Marny. "Half the riders in Australia would give their eye teeth to have had the training you've had."

"I know," replied Marny shyly.

"She is worth the trouble," Tibor told them. "She has helped me too."

It turned out that the men had come to invite Tibor to dine with them at the judges' stand. Tibor was flattered by the recognition, although he doubted if he would ever have the strength to start training seriously again. He left the party with the three distinguished visitors, and Sigi, Trudy, and Charles Cooke-Finch went with them as well.

The stable party ended early, as quite a few of the guests had to compete the next morning. Marny kissed Peter goodnight, excited and flushed. "Wasn't it super those men finding out about Tibor?"

"Yes. But I always wondered why no one knew about him before we found out."

Marny slept deeply and dreamlessly until she woke up to find Candida shaking her. "It's seven o'clock, Marny. Time to get up!" Candida and Barry had arrived the night before, too late to join the party. Candida was thrilled to hear about Marny's success in the first two phases.

"I've got some news for you, too," she said as the two girls started the stable chores together. "I've brought the result of the ketosteroid test Mark asked Professor Metcalfs to do."

"I'd forgotten all about it. What is it? I bet Cas is a rig."

"Right first time."

"It does explain how he gets that extra *oomph*." They began to brush Cas down, one on either side. He clearly enjoyed having two people fussing over him.

"It still amazes me how he's changed," said Candy.

"He's gentle now."

"He hasn't forgotten everything, though. He bit Alex Shooter a couple of days ago."

"He probably deserved it."

By lunchtime all their friends had reassembled at Block E in cheerful anticipation of the show jumping phase that was still to come. Cas had passed the veterinary examination with credit. "I could wish some of the other horses were as fit," the official veterinary officer had told Marny. The scoreboard showed that several horses had been eliminated on veterinary grounds.

Trudy, assuming that no one ever ate properly unless they were at home, was busy dispensing cartons of chocolate milk and piles of meat pies. Peter, Marny and Candida groomed Cas until he was as immaculate as he had been for the dressage phase two days earlier.

"You'd better hurry up and dress, too," Trudy called to her daughter. Marny disappeared into the hay loft with Candida, and fifteen minutes later the two girls reappeared. Marny was smiling rather self-consciously. She looked the very image of an accomplished lady jumper.

Peter gaped with admiration. "What *have* you done to her?"

"Simple. Hair spray, *two* hair nets, and a bit of makeup.

The remaining twenty-one competitors were warming up their horses in the marshalling yards when Marny arrived. They greeted her in friendly tones, recognising her as the newest and youngest competitor to enter the ranks of Three Day Eventers. "I'm glad there aren't many like Alice," thought Marny.

Soon it was time to dismount and walk the course. "Go on. I'll hold the big fellow for you." Peter gave her a comforting hug and Marny followed the others into the arena, where the spectacle of the brightly-coloured jumps belied the seriousness of the competition. No one chatted now. Each rider concentrated on measuring distances and assessing jump heights, and then they all returned slowly and thoughtfully to the marshalling yards. The first horse was called by the red-coated steward. His rider mounted quickly and trotted into the main arena to face the judges and an audience of thousands.

As the competition proceeded, Marny saw that many riders were having a difficult time. The course was a tight and testing one, and some of the horses seemed too fatigued to make that extra effort to clear the obstacles. There were only two clear rounds before she was on.

She saluted and smiled at the plump elderly judge, who returned a friendly nod, making Marny feel much better. The bell rang and Casanova leapt into a canter, ears cocked forward, looking intently towards the starting flags and the first jump. "Easy, boy," she whispered, manoeuvring him around in a circle and setting him on course for the first obstacle. Two stopwatches clicked on as Casanova flashed through the flags. He popped over the brush fence as though it were cavalletti. Racing towards the second jump, a hogsback set at maximum height and width, he lengthened stride and drove forward to leap over it in an athletic parabola.

Half a minute ticked by as they cleared the course faultlessly. The second–last jump was the water, at which Cas had little experience. He was travelling at three-quarter pace coming into the approach but, misjudging the distance, he took off too early. He realised in mid-air that he was not going to land clear, and so he responded by giving a tremendous sideways kick with his hindlegs to give him the required lift. "Good boy," Marny whispered. "Sorry I messed you up." In answer Cas kicked up behind, nearly dislodging Marny from the saddle. The spectators burst into laughter at the big horse's antics. Cas was becoming a showman. Over the final obstacle, a triple bar, and then a sprint through the finish flags. A clear round in plenty of time.

Marny was dismounting in the marshalling yards when a small, wizened figure sidled up to her. Casanova, who had been standing quietly, suddenly laid his ears back. His nostrils flared and he began to prance nervously. Memories came rushing back to him: hateful memories that he could not shake off.

The gates flash open. "They're racing!" The big chestnut colt ducks out a fraction behind the others: the whip cracks down. The colt is maddened. He stops his fast gallop stride and bucks, then rears to his full height. His forelegs paw the air and he gives a piercing stallion scream. The jockey is thrown off and falls almost beneath the flailing hooves. The colt rears again and again. Noise....whips....men....The terrified animal is roped and led away....

"Easy, Toastmaster." The little man spoke firmly and soothingly, but kept a respectful distance. Marny gripped the bridle and caressed Cas's soft muzzle, quietening him.

"I'm sorry," she said, turning to the visitor. "He's still not very used to strangers." Then: *"What* did you call him?"

"Toastmaster!" replied the man cheerily. "And I'm no stranger. He should know me, the old devil. I used to ride 'im, and not so long ago, neither. Look what 'e done to me." He pulled down his T-shirt to display a puckered scar along his collar bone. "They thought I was a goner that time he threw me. But I don't bear 'im no ill-will now. I was real proud of yez out there today. Wished I was ridin' the old devil meself."

"When was it you used to ride him?" asked Marny, her eyes glowing with excitement.

"Four years back, I reckon. 'Is name was Toastmaster in them days. One of the highest-priced neddies ever to come out of

New Zealand. Y' should 'ave seen his pedigree! 'E was descended from Man o' War, and they reckoned 'is bloodlines went back to Hyperion and the Godolphin Arab. I dunno about that. But one thing's sure—if 'e 'adn't bin so vicious, 'e'd 'ave bin another Phar Lap on the Australian turf." He laughed. "Thought I'd done for me that time 'e threw me, though. It was the start of the Golden Slipper Mile for two-year-olds. 'E got barred from the track for life and 'is owner put 'im to run at Stanthorpe."

"That explains it," said Marny. "We're on the direct line from Queensland to Sydney." She smiled at the little man. "Thanks. Thanks a lot for telling me his story. You don't know how much it means to me."

"My pleasure, Missie. Look after 'im well." He patted Casanova on the neck and walked away, soon to be lost in the crowd swarming outside the yards.

"So now we know," said Peter later. "Well, Tibor always thought he must have been a valuable racehorse, and so did Mark. They were right, after all. Eh, Toastmaster?"

"Not Toastmaster. He's Casanova now."

"O.K. Casanova."

They were standing close together, Marny with her right arm around Cas's neck. Peter grasped her other hand and held it tightly. But now their friends were approaching. Tibor and Mrs. Rowbotham, Sigi and Trudy, the Thomases, Charles Cooke-Finch. Everyone was jubilant. "Marny, Peter! Look at the scoreboard!"

They both looked, scarcely believing what they saw. Marny and Casanova had gained second place.

"Congratulations, Marny," said Peter gently. They smiled at one another as their family and friends surrounded them. Marny wanted to cry with her delight.

Tibor took hold of Cas's bridle and they began to walk back to the stable block. "This is your beginning, Marny," he said.

Appendix 1

Tibor Szechy's Training Programme for Marny and Casanova

For Tibor Szechy, the word "dressage" meant far more than simply the physical and mental training of a horse. As he saw it, dressage schooling was a means of improving a horse beyond the stage of plain usefulness, of making him more amenable, easier to control, more pleasant to ride, more graceful in his bearing, and better to look upon. Tibor had spent a lifetime studying the art of dressage and jumping, and he knew that the basic schooling of the talented Casanova was all-important. No short cuts would be taken simply to achieve fast results. The schooling programme would be systematic and balanced to the stage of proficiency attained by both horse and rider as the months went past.

Success in every art depends upon a measure of talent, enthusiasm, hard work, tenacity of purpose, and finally on a sound knowledge of the principles involved in that art. Tibor Szechy was well aware that the equestrian art, perhaps more than any other, is closely related to the philosophy of life itself. Many of the basic principles of schooling can also be applied to human beings as examples of wise conduct. They teach us self control, constancy, and the ability to understand the feelings and reactions of another living creature. From his relationship with his horse the rider will learn that only kindness and mutual understanding will bring about achievement.

Marny soon realised that to attain her goal of Three Day Eventing, she must devote to riding and schooling all her mental and physical abilities.

The schooling of a young horse may be arbitrarily divided into three phases. Phase One involves "riding forward," or riding the horse with a natural carriage on straight lines in the ordinary paces. The movement is free and forward, both with the rein in contact and with a long rein. In Phase Two, the horse, now "on the bit," is ridden in turns and circles at all paces and in correct balance. Cross-country riding and jumping can be developed at this point. During this phase of schooling the horse's natural impulsion, carriage, and paces are built upon and improved. His proficiency and stamina will be increased and his intelligence and understanding awakened. The second phase of riding has to be developed from the first, which in turn prepares the horse for Phase Three. During the last phase the horse is ridden regularly in greater collection, bringing him to a peak of suppleness and proficiency. He is also trained to increase the bend in the joints of the hindlegs at all ordinary paces. These movements, developed by training to the highest degree of skill, comprise what is known as "high school."

When Casanova was ready to enter the Three Day Event at the Sydney Royal Show, he had nearly completed Phase Two of his schooling.

Appendix 2

Casanova's Feeding Programme

As a vet, Mark Thomas had the knowledge to work out a balanced ration to feed Casanova from the time when he was a thin, out-of-condition horse, up to the point where he was fit and ready to compete in a Three Day Event. To do this, he relied on several basic premises to help him decide what to feed Cas, when to feed him, and how to feed him.

First, he realised that the various feeds for horses contain different amounts of energy. For example, corn contains about twenty percent more energy than oats, which contains about thirty percent more energy than oaten chaff. It is vital to be aware of the energy values of foodstuffs and to feed horses according to their energy needs alone. These needs are calculated on (a) the live weight of the horse and (b) the amount of work it performs.

Many other factors will of course influence these basic energy requirements: these include the type of work the horse is doing, the steepness of the terrain on which he is working, climatic conditions, and the horse's own temperament. A nervous, highly-strung horse will burn up more energy for his basic maintenance requirements than a less excitable animal of similar body weight.

The following important rules must be considered in any successful feeding programme:

1. Always feed your horse as an individual.
2. Feed him little and often. A horse's digestive system is not adapted to one large feed a day. Horses fed large amounts of concentrates (for example, Three Day Event horses) may have to be given several small feeds a day. This will ensure that all feeds are consumed and that the horse maintains a keen appetite.
3. Feed him at regular intervals. This applies not only to week days, but to holidays and weekends as well.
4. Feed him only the best quality feeding-stuffs available. The energy values of most feeds drop drastically with the decline in quality.
5. Observe your horse's feed, feed residue, and faeces daily. This will tell you much about his general health.
6. Water should be available to your horse at all times.
7. Feed concentrates carefully. There are several points to watch here:
   (a) Do not introduce grain too rapidly into your horse's diet.
   (b) Substitute grain for bulk feed on an energy basis.
   (c) Restrict grain on idle days. (Many horse-owners forget to do this, and they can pay dearly for such carelessness. A common result of such overfeeding is azoturia— a painful and dangerous condition.)
   (d) Do not allow your horse to eat his grain ration too rapidly.

Protein forms an important constituent in the rations of young, growing horses as well as pregnant and lactating mares. However, the amount of protein required for the maintenance of the mature horse is normally covered in any ration feed that has been balanced for energy requirements.

Mineral nutrients are essential for the general health of all animals, and for many years the importance of common salt (sodium chloride), calcium, and phosphorus in horse-feeding has been recognised. Salt is the most common essential mineral and should be included in the ration at the rate of 0·5 percent by weight of the ration. Calcium, phosphorus, and vitamin D are closely related in their effect on the well-being of the horse. He must receive adequate amounts of sunlight if he is to reach his vitamin D requirement, and a mature horse should also receive a balanced amount of calcium and phosphorus in the ratio of 1·2:1 (calcium: phosphorus).

The ration devised by Mark Thomas for Casanova in the early stages of his training, when his live-weight was 500 kilograms (1100 pounds) was:

Feeding stuff	Kilograms
Oats	3 (7 pounds)
Oaten chaff	2 (4 pounds)
Bran	1 (2 pounds)
Linseed meal	0–25 (0–5 pounds)
Lucerne hay	2–3 (5 pounds)

This was supplemented by 1–5 tablespoons of common salt, 1–3 tablespoons of limestone powder, and light grazing in a small paddock. The ration was gradually increased, depending on Casanova's live-weight gains and on the amount of work he had to perform as his training progressed and his work-load became more and more demanding. By the time he was ready for the Three Day Event, fourteen months after Marny had acquired him, he gained considerably in condition and muscle, and weighed 590 kilograms (1300 pounds). His ration was now:

Feeding stuff	Kilograms
Oats	8 (18 pounds)
Oaten chaff	1 (2 pounds)
Bran	0–7 (1–5 pounds)
Linseed meal	0–5 (1 pound)
Lucerne hay	2 (4 pounds)

In addition, his ration now included 2–5 tablespoons of common salt, 5 tablespoons of limestone powder, and light grazing in a small paddock.

In devising the final ration for Casanova for the Three Day Event, Mark Thomas had to consider aspects other than pure energy, protein, mineral, and vitamin requirements. For horses in strenuous training, nutrition interacts with many other factors, including temperament, conformation, soundness, general health, and work performed by muscles in training. All these things have an effect on whether or not the horse will reach his peak of fitness.